DINNER WITH THE
FISHWIFE

Dinner with the
FISHWIFE

Rachel McGlashan

NEW HOLLAND

DEDICATION

Firstly, to the three most important men in my life …

My husband Al, my inspiration, my motivation, my best friend and my love; your passion inspires me every day.

To my sons Thomas and Cooper, my pride and joys, my reason for everything, I love you 'to infinity and beyond!'

To my Mum and Dad, who have always been there, with love, support, friendship and encouragement and sometimes a good old clip around the ears. You mean the world to me and you have dedicated your lives to raising your family, working tirelessly and never complaining. I hope this book goes some way in showing you just how well you did!

To my Nan and Pop; I love and miss you.

ACKNOWLEDGEMENTS

To Fiona at New Holland, thank you for this opportunity. Thank you for understanding also just who and what I have to live with!

To all the team at New Holland, you guys are the ultimate professionals, thanks it was a blast!

To Graeme Gillies, I immensely enjoyed working with you; you are the second best photographer I've worked with (Al made me say that!).

To Susan and Gran, thank you for all your support, not just to us as a family, but to myself over the years.

To Sylvie, the best neighbour anyone could ask for and the best 'Nan in lieu' my kids could ever have. Thank you.

Most importantly, to all my willing (and perhaps not so willing!) taste testers … There are too many of you to mention, but you know who you are. I appreciate and thank you for your friendship and support and for putting your lives into my hands!

A special thank you to the Rushbys—Craig, Kath, Brad and Corinne, thank you for the lazy days by your dam. To Mick, a true friend, thanks for 'Reel Diamond'. And to my niece Leah, who shares a love of cooking, thank you for coming to Sydney and helping me. I hope we can share many more cooking, eating and drinking times together!

CONTENTS

INTRODUCTION

I don't think anyone, least of all myself, ever expected I would produce a fish cookbook. But, as it often does, life threw me a curve ball in the shape of Al, my husband! His love and passion for fishing soon encompassed our life. Realistically, it was only a matter of time before I too became wrapped up in a life of fishing. Who I was before Al and who I am now are poles apart, and thus my life journey has also taken quite a change in direction.

Before I met Al, not only had I never been fishing but I was lucky if I ate fish once or twice a year—on Good Friday and whenever we had fish and chips! How that has all changed! I now fish with him (though not as often now we have two kids!). We also eat beautiful, fresh fish four or five nights a week, from kingfish and tuna to snapper and mahi mahi. I am spoilt and I am the first to admit it! I am kept in fish luxury!

This brings with it many challenges—how do I cook fish every night and still keep it interesting?

With two young boys, who seem to be taking after their Dad, keeping the cooking interesting has been a challenge. Time is precious these days and like all mums I don't have the time to cook fancy meals that take all day. I want to walk into that kitchen (mine is actually more akin to a 'dog box'—yes it's that small!) and be serving up in as little time as possible! On occasion I need to take some extra special care and turn out something a bit more grand, so I have included a few of these too.

Over the years I have built up a collection of recipes that my family and friends love. My inspiration comes from the vast variety of fresh food available to us, as well as the abundance of talented chefs we have here in Australia. I am no chef. I am a mother and a fisherman's wife, and what I do well is to use what I have available to me—and that is a lot of fresh fish!

Buying fresh fish can be a daunting task if you don't have the ability to catch it yourself. It is little wonder that a lot of people don't like fish, or dislike cooking with it. When we don't know what to buy, it is hard to make a well-informed decision. We baulk at spending alot on seafood and so all the best quality Australian fish is exported. As a result we get the leftovers and more often than not inferior imported fish, which is absurd for a country surrounded by such rich seas.

I offered someone some fresh bluefin tuna recently (one of the most expensive table fishes in the world mind you!) that Al had caught only three days earlier off Bermagui (on the south coast of NSW). I was turned down, not because they didn't eat fish, but because they didn't cook fish at home because of the smell! I was gobsmacked, and really wasn't sure how to respond. How do you prove to someone that fresh fish doesn't smell like week-old frozen fish?

The key to getting the freshest fish you can is to buy local fish that is in season. Look for whole fish that is fresh with shiny scales and eyes that are clean. Where you can, buy whole fish and ask the fishmonger to fillet it for you (if they are a good fishmonger they will do it for you!). Don't go into the fish shop with a particular fish in mind, go in with a budget and buy the best and freshest local fish you can for your money. This is why it is important to find a fishmonger who always stocks fresh fish, get to know them and always look at what you are buying before ordering. My best advice though, would be to go and get a rod and reel as well as a fishing licence and go and catch your own!

You will notice as you read my recipes that I don't always state a particular fish to use. That is because I never look at that, I cook with what I have—be adventurous. Second, I find that fish are interchangeable; one fish can always be substituted for another. Have a look at the Knowing Your Fish table at the back of the book. Don't get locked in by what type of fish a recipe calls for, it may not be available, or in season, it may not be local product guaranteeing you quality and it may not be something you know all your family will love to eat.

The first thing is to realise that while deep-frying fish in batter is one way, there are so many other ways to enjoy fish! Fish is one of the healthier choices we can make. We don't baulk at spending good money on meat or chicken, we shouldn't skimp on our budget with fish either. If more of us demanded good, fresh, local fish, we may just be able to get that, instead of frozen imported stuff!

I know you will enjoy this book. More importantly, enjoy your fish!

Rachel McGlashan
Working hard so Al can fish hard!
www.almcglashan.com/fishwife

This is me (centre) doing what I love best: cooking for Al (far left) and our family and friends!

Seasonal availability of species

Main fisheries

Spring

Jewfish	NSW
Kingfish	NSW
Bonito	NSW
Silver Trevally	NSW
Leatherjackets	NSW
Tuna	NSW, Qld
Bream	NSW, Qld, Vic, Tas
Blue Swimmer crabs	NSW, WA, Qld
Squid	NSW, Vic, Tas, SA, WA
Tailor	NSW, Qld, WA
Sand Whiting	NSW, Qld
School prawns	NSW, Qld, eastern Vic, WA
King Prawns	Qld, NSW, Vic
Threadfin	Qld, NT
Mud crabs	Qld, NT, WA
Barramundi	Qld, NT, WA
Snapper	Vic, NSW, SA, WA
Flathead	Vic, Qld, SA, Tas
Spanish Mackerel	WA, NT, Qld
Golden Snapper	NT
Black Jewfish	NT

Summer

Bream	NSW, Qld, Vic, Tas
Jewfish	NSW
Tuna	NSW, Tas
Kingfish	NSW
Bonito	NSW
Squid	NSW, Vic, Tas, SA, WA
Silver Trevally	NSW, Vic, WA
Tailor	NSW, WA
Sand Whiting	NSW, Qld
King George Whiting	WA, SA, Vic
Leatherjackets	NSW, Vic
Blue Swimmer crabs	NSW, WA, Qld
Barramundi	Qld, WA, NT
Mud crabs	Qld, NT, WA, NSW
School prawns	Qld, NSW, eastern Vic. WA
Flathead	Vic, Qld, SA, Tas
Australian salmon	Vic, SA, WA, Tas
Snapper	Vic, SA, WA

Autumn

Bream	NSW, Qld, Vic, Tas
Blue Grenadier	NSW, Vic, Tas
Jewfish	NSW
Squid	NSW, Vic, Tas, SA, WA
Tuna	NSW, Tas
Kingfish	NSW
Bonito	NSW
Silver Trevally	NSW, Vic, WA
Leatherjackets	NSW
Ling	NSW
Blue Swimmer crabs	NSW, WA, Qld
Coral Trout	Qld
Barramundi	Qld, NT, WA
School prawns	Qld, NSW, eastern Vic, WA
Snapper	Vic, SA, WA, NSW
Flathead	Vic, Qld, SA, Tas, NSW
Australian Salmon	Vic, SA, WA, Tas

Winter

Bream	NSW, Qld, Vic
John Dory	NSW
Tuna	NSW, Qld
Snapper	NSW, Southern Qld
Jewfish	NSW, Southern Qld
Squid	NSW, Vic, Tas, SA, WA
Blue Grenadier	NSW, Vic, Tas
Kingfish	NSW, Southern Qld
Bonito	NSW
Silver Trevally	NSW
Leatherjackets	NSW
Coral Trout	Qld
Spanish Mackerel	Qld, WA, NT,
King prawns	Qld, NSW, Vic
Flathead	Vic, Qld, NSW
Ling	Vic, NSW

Note

A lot of these species are available year round but I have only highlighted the peak season. Always consult your fishmonger—the fish don't always run exactly to the season!

CARING FOR YOUR CATCH

Catching fish is one thing but you also need to work hard to keep the fish in prime condition for the table. Over the years I have had a lot of people tell me they don't like eating fish. However, after eating the fish I have given them they have all come back saying that it is the best fish they have ever eaten. There is no magic remedy, instead I simply look after my catch and then serve it fresh. This is a far cry from the fish you get at the fish shop which can take more than two weeks to reach the table.

Fish has a delicate flesh and the quality deteriorates rapidly if it isn't cared for properly. The only way to ensure the fish is fresh in my books is to go and catch it yourself.

So what do we need to do to ensure the fish we catch reaches the plate in the best possible condition? The first step is to dispatch the fish humanely and then gut the fish. This may sound gruesome but it is all part of the deal and will increase the quality of the meat considerably. Some fish like tuna, shark and mackerel, which have a high blood count, need to be bled thoroughly, while for other fish like snapper and flathead it is less essential. I should also add that you shouldn't let the fish kick around on the deck because this will often tear its muscles which makes the flesh flaky.

Don't leave your fish on the deck in the sun. After bleeding the fish get it on ice fast. I like to carry an esky loaded with crushed ice; that way I can bury the fish and cool it down quickly for perfect quality meat. There is simply no excuse for poor quality fish if you catch it yourself. Especially when you consider the time and expense you went to to catch it.

Preparing your catch for the table

Different fish require different styles of filleting to maximise fillet size whilst removing bones. A super sharp knife is essential and if you are inexperienced a chain mail glove may be worthwhile to ensure you keep all your fingers!

Filleting hints
- Set up a decent cutting board that is easy to work around.
- Keep the workstation clean by regularly washing it down to minimise contamination.
- Keep knives razor sharp and have a sharpening tool on hand.

Boneless flathead tail fillets

1. Holding the fish on its side by the head, scale it by running the knife from the tail up towards the head. A couple of scrapes with the knife will do the job.
2. With the fish scaled, keep holding the fish on its side and place the knife across the fish at the end of the rib cage.
3. Run the knife down through the fillet to the backbone.
4. Turn the knife horizontal to the backbone and cut to the tail.
5. At this point I like to complete the fillet by slicing it off at the tail resulting in a beautiful boneless fillet. Rinse in a bucket of salt water to clean and it is ready for cooking.
6. If you prefer to skin the fillet then don't bother scaling it and instead of finishing the fillet off leave the end of the skin attached at the tail. Lay the fillet over, then run the knife down between the skin and the fillet. The two should part fairly easy resulting in a boneless and skinless fillet.

Gutting a snapper

1. Scale the fish using a heavy-duty metal scaler (snapper have larger coarser scales than flathead and they are hard to remove with a filleting knife).
2. Holding the fish upside down, run the knife from the bum right up to the throat latch at the base of the gills.
3. Cut the top of the throat latch and then break the gills away from the sides and then rip them out by pushing your thumb in behind at the top of them and pull down, ripping them free.
4. With the gills free you can pull them back down the gut cavity, removing the guts in one swift move.
5. Remove any remnants from the gut cavity and run the knife along the backbone to clean out the blood line.
6. Wash the fish in salt water and you're ready for cooking.

Filleting a kingfish

1. Holding the fish firmly on its side, run the knife in against the dorsal fin and run it along the spine to the back of the head. Then repeat the process by running the knife the opposite way to the tail.
2. Insert the knife in behind the pectoral fin and run it up behind the head to meet up with the previous cut, then run it down across the belly to the end of the gut cavity and then follow the backbone up to the tail.
3. Turn the fish over and repeat the process.

4. Now lifting the fillet either side slide the knife through at the anal fin then run it down over the spine to the tail cutting the fillet away from the backbone. Holding the fillet in one hand run the knife up to the head, cutting the fillet away from the backbone in the.

5. Repeat the process on the other side. If you see you have left a bit of meat on the frame simply slice it off—no point in wasting it!

6. Lay the fillet skin down and then run the knife up the centre, either side of the blood line and bones.

7. The next step is to put the knife in the cut at the top of the fillet and slice the meat away from the skin. You can make the job easier by lifting the fillet as you work with the knife.

8. Repeat on the other side and you will have two boneless and skinless fillets ready for the barbie.

Kindly contributed by Al McGlashan

Cooking your fish

The one rule that you need to remember is to not OVERCOOK your fish. How do you do this? Your fish will go from a translucent look to being completely opaque. It's ready!

One way I always use to check is by putting a fork into the fleshiest part of the fish and if, when you gently move the fork, the flesh flakes away easily—it is cooked. If it is a whole fish or a cutlet, the flesh will flake easily away from the bone.

I have also included a recipe for smoked fish and how to smoke it. Try it! It's out of this world!

Something I can't live without is my Cobb portable stove. It runs on compressed coconut shell, and you can carry it anywhere, even when it's hot. There's a picture of it in the Barbie, Boat or Beach section.

Tips for freezing fish

Freezing fish correctly is a real art form and requires a lot of skill to do it correctly. Some fish species like kingfish freeze really well, while others such as threadfin salmon are terrible and go mushy when defrosted. So the first step is to determine which species freeze best. As a general rule firm fillets or whole fish like snapper freeze well. If you are unsure ask your local fishmonger or fishing expert for advice.

Once the fillets are ready, place them in freezer bags and then dip the bag in a sink full of cold water. This will instantly remove all the air out of the bag. Then simply wrap it tightly around the fillets to seal. The reason for getting the air out is because it causes freezer burn and shortens the lifespan of the meat. Alternatively, if you are freezing fish whole then one trick is not to scale them as the scales will offer extra protection, although it can be hard to scale after defrosting.

If you're really serious about looking after your fillets then get a purpose-built food saver that sucks all the air out and seals the bags automatically. This takes a bit of effort and the special bags aren't cheap but you will end up with the best possible quality fillets around.

BREKKIE & BRUNCH

Bacon, Mushroom and Fish Parcels

A great recipe for breakfast or brunch.

1 TABLESPOON OLIVE OIL

15G UNSALTED BUTTER

3 SHALLOTS, FINELY
 CHOPPED

200G MUSHROOMS (YOUR
 CHOICE, I LIKE TO USE A
 MIX), FINELY CHOPPED

200G FISH (ONCE AGAIN
 YOUR CHOICE, WHATEVER
 YOU HAVE AT HAND), FINELY
 CHOPPED

40G BREADCRUMBS

2 TABLESPOONS CRÈME
 FRAICHE

2 EGG YOLKS

¼ CUP CONTINENTAL
 PARSLEY, FINELY CHOPPED

SALT AND PEPPER

1 DOZEN RASHERS OF BACON,
 RIND OFF

Preheat the oven to 200°C. Heat the oil and butter in a frypan, add the shallots and cook till they soften. Add the mushrooms and fish. Cook for 5 more minutes until the mushrooms are softened and the fish is just cooked. Drain away any liquid and cool.

Add to the fish mixture the breadcrumbs, crème fraiche, egg yolks, parsley, and salt and pepper, and combine to form the 'stuffing'. Line 6 ramekins (or a large muffin tin) with 2 slices of bacon per ramekin, lay the bacon down in a cross. Spoon stuffing in, press down and fold the bacon over the top. Bake in the oven for 20 minutes.

Heat the grill. Remove the parcels from the oven, run a knife around the edge of each, and turn them out. Place under the grill, just for a few minutes until the bacon on top is golden.

Serves 6

Pear, Fig and Kingfish Tart

SPRAY OLIVE OIL
12-15 SHEETS OF FILO PASTRY
½ CUP BREADCRUMBS
2 KINGFISH FILLETS, THINLY
  SLICED
4 PEARS, CORED, PEELED AND
  FINELY SLICED
I TEASPOON BROWN SUGAR
4 DRIED FIGS, PUREED
¼ CUP HONEY
DASH OF MUSCAT

Preheat oven to 200°C.

Spray a baking tray with olive oil. Lay out the filo pastry on the bench and cut in half into two rectangles. Take one sheet of filo and lay on the baking tray and spray with oil. Repeat this process. For every third sheet sprinkle some breadcrumbs over the filo before spraying with olive oil. After 12-15 sheets, fold over the edges of filo about 1 cm and spray edges with oil.

Starting with a slice of fish, alternate the fish and pear, overlapping them in rows on top of the filo.

Place a small frypan over a moderate heat, combine figs, honey and muscat. Heat through, stirring constantly. Pour evenly over the prepared tart and place in oven.

Cook for 10-15 minutes or until filo is golden brown.

Serves 6

Fish and Dill Savoury Tarts

Combine the stock and cream and set aside. Heat oil over a medium–high heat. Add the leek and cook for 5 minutes or until soft then add the flour and cook, stirring for 1 minute more. Pour in the stock/cream mix to pan and bring to the boil. Reduce the heat and stir through the mustard until combined. Add the fish and dill and simmer for 3 to 5 minutes until the fish is just cooked through.

Preheat grill on medium high. Spoon the mixture into pastry shells, top with breadcrumbs and grill for 5 minutes or until lightly browned. Serve on a platter sprinkled with dill.

Makes 24

1½ CUPS FISH STOCK
½ CUP CREAM
2 TABLESPOONS OLIVE OIL
1 LEEK, FINELY SLICED
2 TABLESPOONS PLAIN FLOUR
2 TABLESPOONS DIJON MUSTARD
600G FISH, DICED
¼ CUP DILL, FINELY CHOPPED
24 PRE-BAKED SAVOURY PASTRY SHELLS (YOU COULD MAKE YOUR OWN IF YOU ARE BRAVE OR THEY ALSO WORK WELL IN VOL-AU-VENT CASES)
2 TABLESPOONS BREADCRUMBS

Kingfish and Asparagus Frittata

In a medium bowl, cover asparagus with boiling water and leave for 1 minute. Run under cold water to halt cooking process and drain well. Whisk eggs and cream together and season with salt and pepper.

Preheat grill (remember to lower rack before it gets hot—it tends to be easier this way!). Melt butter in frypan (use one that can go under the grill) over medium to high heat. Add leek and capers and cook until leek is just softened. Add asparagus, kingfish, dill and mint and stir to combine. Pour egg over. Reduce heat to medium to low. Cook for 2 to 3 minutes until base is set.

Place under the grill until top is golden and set. Turn out onto plate and slice into wedges. Garnish with extra dill and mint.

Serves 4-6

1 BUNCH ASPARAGUS, TRIMMED AND SLICED ON THE DIAGONAL
6 EGGS, LIGHTLY WHISKED
$1/3$ CUP THICKENED CREAM
SALT AND PEPPER, TO TASTE
20G BUTTER
1 LEEK, FINELY SLICED
1 TABLESPOON CAPERS, RINSED AND CHOPPED
300G KINGFISH, STEAMED OR POACHED, AND BROKEN UP WITH A FORK
$1/4$ CUP FRESH DILL, CHOPPED
2 TABLESPOONS MINT LEAVES, SHREDDED

Tuna Stuffed Baby Capsicum

300G TUNA
6 RED BABY CAPSICUMS
½ CUP BREADCRUMBS
2 TABLESPOONS BUTTER,
  MELTED
½ ROUND WHEEL OF BRIE,
  CHOPPED ROUGHLY
¼ CUP CHIVES, FINELY
  CHOPPED
¼ CUP LEMON THYME,
  FINELY CHOPPED
SALT AND PEPPER, TO SEASON
LEMON WEDGES, TO SERVE

Heat oven to 200°C. Using a bamboo steamer, steam tuna over a low heat until just cooked. Remove from steamer and allow to cool.

Using a small sharp knife cut stem off each capsicum and remove seeds and pith, leaving the skin whole. Line baking tray with baking paper and place capsicums on the baking tray.

In a small bowl, mix the breadcrumbs and melted butter and set aside. Place brie, chives, lemon thyme and seasoning in a bowl with the tuna. Break up the tuna with a fork and mix. Spoon into capsicum skins, top with breadcrumb mix and cook in the oven for approximately 10-15 minutes. You want the capsicums to be gently roasted but not so they are collapsing.

TIP: You can also steam the fish in the microwave or even poach it.

Serves 6 (as entrée)

REEL DIAMOND

Fish Omelette with Hoisin Sauce

I use 5 eggs in this omelette. This is just personal, we love a thicker egg base and because I can never get the flipping right we sometimes bypass that part and just slide the omelette whole onto a plate. This is also a full meal. If you want to make it into a lighter snack, just use 2-3 eggs.

Whisk the eggs and water together in a bowl. Heat the oil over a medium-high heat in a small frypan. Add the egg mix, tilting pan to ensure mix covers the bottom and sides of pan. Keep lifting the edge as the omelette cooks. This will allow the still 'runny' egg to run underneath and cook. Cook until nearly set, then top with fish, capsicum, spring onion and coriander.

When omelette is set, fold over and slide onto a plate. Drizzle with hoisin sauce and serve.

TIP: If you are going to leave the omelette whole and not flip it over, I like to give it a minute or two under a grill.

Serves 1

5 EGGS
¼ CUP WATER
1 TABLESPOON PEANUT OIL
100G PRESERVED FISH (SEE PAGE 186) OR 100G FRESH FISH, GRILLED LIGHTLY AND FLAKED
¼ RED CAPSICUM, FINELY DICED
1 SPRING ONION, FINELY SLICED
¼ CUP CORIANDER, FINELY CHOPPED
HOISIN SAUCE

Fish Crepes

¼ CUP HOISIN SAUCE

2 TEASPOONS RICE VINEGAR

8 CREPES (FROM THE FROZEN
  FOODS SECTION OF YOUR
  SUPERMARKET OR MAKE
  YOUR OWN)

3 CUPS COOKED FISH,
  SHREDDED (I EITHER GRILL
  OR STEAM MY FISH)

3 SPRING ONIONS, CUT INTO
  5CM LENGTHS

I CUCUMBER, JULIENNED

HANDFUL OF CHIVES, FINELY
  CHOPPED

Combine hoisin sauce and rice vinegar. In microwave heat crepes as per instructions on packet. Lay a crepe out, spread with 1 teaspoon of hoisin mix, add fish, spring onion, cucumber and sprinkle of chives.

Roll up and cut in half. Repeat for each crepe.

Makes 8 crepes

WARMING SOUPS

Fish, Sweet Potato and Coriander Soup

1 TABLESPOON PEANUT OIL

2 LEEKS, FINELY SLICED

4 CLOVES GARLIC, CRUSHED

4 CUPS CHICKEN STOCK

2 MEDIUM SWEET POTATOES
 (ABOUT 800G TOTAL),
 SLICED

500G FISH, CUBED SMALL OR
 MINCED

2/3 CUP LIGHT EVAPORATED
 MILK

1/3 CUP CORIANDER LEAVES

2 TABLESPOONS
 WORCESTERSHIRE SAUCE

Heat the oil in a saucepan. Cook the leeks and garlic, stirring, until the leek is soft. Add the chicken stock and sweet potato. Bring to the boil, then reduce heat, cover and simmer until the potato is soft.

Blend the soup in a food processor until smooth then return to simmer, add fish and cook until it thickens slightly. Stir in the evaporated milk, coriander and Worcestershire sauce. Stir through and heat without boiling.

The soup is ready to eat when the fish is cooked through. Garnish with extra fresh coriander.

Serves 4-6

Cream of Fish Soup

Melt the butter in large saucepan, add onion and garlic and cook until soft, approximately 3 to 4 minutes. Add fish and cook for 1 to 2 minutes more. Pour in stock and milk and bring to boil. Reduce heat to simmer and cook for 5 minutes. Cool slightly, pour into blender and process till smooth. Return to pan over a low heat, adding the cream. Season with salt and pepper.

Preheat oven to 180°C. Crumb the baguette and garlic in a food processor. Spread on a baking tray and toast for 5 to 6 minutes until golden brown, then toss with parsley.

Divide soup between serving bowls and top with crumb mix.

Serves 4-6

SOUP
50G UNSALTED BUTTER

1 ONION, FINELY DICED

3 CLOVES GARLIC, CRUSHED

400G FISH FILLETS, CUBED

2 CUPS CHICKEN STOCK

300ML MILK

300ML CREAM

GARLIC BREADCRUMBS
1 SMALL BAGUETTE

1 CLOVE GARLIC

SMALL HANDFUL FLAT LEAF PARSLEY, FINELY CHOPPED

Fish Noodle Soup

Cook noodles according to packet directions, drain and set aside. Heat the olive oil in a saucepan over a medium-high heat. Add the leek, fennel, garlic, ginger, chilli and coriander (roots and stems). Cook for 4 to 5 minutes until leek and fennel are tender. Add the celery, capsicum and mushrooms and cook for a further 2 minutes. Pour in the stock and lime juice and bring to the boil. Reduce heat and add fish and simmer for 5 minutes. Add the pak choy, simmer for a further 2 minutes or until pak choy has just started to wilt. Turn off heat and stir through the coriander and mint leaves.

Divide noodles between 4 serving bowls, pour over the soup and garnish with fried shallots or onions to serve.

Serves 4

1 PACKET UDON NOODLES
2 TABLESPOONS OLIVE OIL
1 LEEK, FINELY SLICED
1 BABY FENNEL BULB, FINELY SLICED
2 GARLIC CLOVES, CRUSHED
3CM PIECE GINGER, JULIENNED
1 LONG RED CHILLI, DESEEDED AND FINELY SLICED
1 BUNCH CORIANDER, ROOTS AND STEMS FINELY CHOPPED (LEAVES ROUGHLY CHOPPED AND KEPT SEPARATE)
2 STALKS CELERY, FINELY SLICED
1 RED CAPSICUM, FINELY SLICED
50G MUSHROOMS, QUARTERED
4 CUPS CHICKEN STOCK
1 LIME, JUICED
500G FISH, FINELY SLICED
1 BUNCH BABY PAK CHOY, QUARTERED
4 SPRIGS OF MINT, LEAVES ONLY

OPTIONAL: FRIED SHALLOTS OR ONIONS TO GARNISH

Easy Fish Laksa

125G RICE NOODLES
3 CUPS CHICKEN STOCK
140ML COCONUT MILK
1 TABLESPOON CURRY
  PASTE (SELECT YOUR OWN
  FLAVOUR)
1 TABLESPOON KAFFIR LIME
  LEAVES, CHOPPED ROUGHLY
1 LEMONGRASS STALK,
  BRUISED AND FINELY
  CHOPPED
250G FISH, FINELY SLICED
10-12 PRAWNS, COOKED,
  SHELLED, HEADS ON OR OFF
  DEPENDING ON PREFERENCE
4 BABY BOK CHOY,
  QUARTERED

Cook noodles as per instructions on packet and set aside.

Combine stock, coconut milk, curry paste, Kaffir lime and lemongrass in a large saucepan. Bring to the boil, stirring occasionally. Reduce to low heat and simmer for 3 minutes.

Stir in the fish and simmer for a further 3 minutes. Add prawns and bok choy and simmer for 1 minute more. Divide noodles between 4 bowls. Remove lime leaves and lemongrass if preferred. Pour soup over the top and serve.

Serves 4

Coconut and Lemongrass Fish Soup

4 CUPS CHICKEN STOCK
270ML COCONUT MILK
10CM FRESH LEMONGRASS
  STICK, FINELY CHOPPED
2 HEAPED TEASPOONS
  CRUSHED GINGER
1 HEAPED TEASPOON
  CRUSHED GARLIC
2 TEASPOONS FISH SAUCE
600G FISH, THINLY SLICED
300G OYSTER MUSHROOMS,
  HALVED
1 LONG RED CHILLI, FINELY
  SLICED
1 TABLESPOON LIME JUICE
4 SPRING ONIONS, THINLY
  SLICED

In a saucepan combine chicken stock, coconut milk, lemongrass, ginger, garlic and fish sauce. Bring to the boil then reduce heat, cover and simmer for 10 minutes. Add the fish, mushrooms, chilli and lime juice and bring back to the boil. Reduce heat, cover and simmer until fish is cooked. Serve garnished with spring onion.

Serves 4-6

Lime Fish Soup

Put fish and stock in saucepan and bring to boil. Reduce heat and simmer for 5 minutes until the fish is cooked through, then remove from the heat and set aside.

In another saucepan heat the oil over a medium heat. Add the corn and capsicum and cook for about 2 minutes until the capsicum is tender. Add the tomato, cumin and oregano and cook for another 2 minutes until the tomato is soft. Add the fish and stock, lime juice and lime slices. Bring to a simmer, then season with salt and pepper.

Serve topped with coriander, spring onions and feta.

500G FISH, CUT INTO LARGE CUBES

4 CUPS CHICKEN STOCK

1 TABLESPOON OLIVE OIL

1 CORN COB, HUSK AND SILKS REMOVED AND CORN SLICED FROM COB (OR 1 CUP CANNED SWEET CORN, DRAINED)

1 GREEN CAPSICUM, DE-SEEDED AND FINELY CHOPPED

2 RIPE ROMA TOMATOES, FINELY CHOPPED

1 TEASPOON GROUND CUMIN

1 TEASPOON DRIED OREGANO

2 TABLESPOONS LIME JUICE

1 LIME, THINLY SLICED

1 CUP CORIANDER LEAVES, ROUGHLY CHOPPED

4 SPRING ONIONS/SHALLOTS, THINLY SLICED

100G FETA CHEESE, CRUMBLED

Tomato and Chilli Fish Soup

2 TABLESPOONS OLIVE OIL
350G FISH FILLETS
1 RED ONION, FINELY
  CHOPPED
1 TABLESPOON FLOUR
6 CUPS STOCK (I PREFER
  CHICKEN STOCK BUT YOU
  COULD USE VEGETABLE OR
  FISH INSTEAD)
2 CUPS TOMATO JUICE
420G CAN CORN KERNELS,
  DRAINED
1 LARGE RED CHILLI,
  DESEEDED AND FINELY
  CHOPPED
¼ CUP FRESH CORIANDER
  LEAVES (BE GENEROUS)

Heat half of the oil in a large saucepan and cook fish. Remove from pan and allow to cool. Break into smaller pieces.

Reheat the oil and cook the onion till soft. Add flour to the onion and stir until it thickens. Gradually stir in the stock and the tomato juice. Cook, stirring until the liquid boils and thickens slightly. Add corn and chilli and stir through. Add fish and stir until hot. Sprinkle with coriander just before serving.

Serves 4

Thai-style Fish Soup

I have been making this soup for years, and while it takes a lot of ingredients, which I don't normally like, once they are organised it is easy to make. The whole reason to bother is because it tastes fantastic!

Heat oil in a large saucepan and fry the leek and garlic until soft. Add curry powder, cumin and ground coriander and stir until fragrant. Add the fish to the pan and cook until the fish is slightly golden.

Bruise the lemongrass by applying pressure with the flat of a knife and squashing. Cut in half. In a saucepan, bring the stock, lemongrass, coconut milk and sambal to the boil, reduce the heat and simmer for 10 minutes.

Mix cornflour and water together in a cup and stir into the soup. Add the fish sauce. Bring soup to boil then reduce to a simmer. Add capsicum, spring onions, lime juice and fresh coriander and serve.

Serves 6

1 TABLESPOON PEANUT OIL
1 LEEK, FINELY SLICED
2 TEASPOONS GARLIC, MINCED
1 TEASPOON MILD CURRY
 POWDER
1 TEASPOON GROUND CUMIN
½ TEASPOON GROUND
 CORIANDER
500G FISH FILLETS, CUT INTO
 STRIPS
1 STEM FRESH LEMONGRASS
4 CUPS CHICKEN STOCK (OR
 FISH STOCK)
1 2/3 CUPS OF COCONUT MILK
2 TEASPOONS SAMBAL OELEK
1 TABLESPOON CORNFLOUR
1 TABLESPOON WATER
1 TEASPOON FISH SAUCE
1 SMALL RED CAPSICUM,
 THINLY SLICED
4 SPRING ONIONS, FINELY
 SLICED
1 TABLESPOON LIME JUICE
½ BUNCH CORIANDER, FINELY
 CHOPPED

LIGHT BITES

Warm Thai Herb Salad

½ CUP BASIL LEAVES

½ CUP MINT LEAVES

1/3 CUP CORIANDER

2 SPRING ONIONS/SHALLOTS, FINELY SLICED

2 TABLESPOONS PEANUT OIL

600G FISH FILLETS (FIRM FLESH), THINLY SLICED

2 GARLIC CLOVES, CRUSHED

3CM PIECE OF GINGER, PEELED AND FINELY CHOPPED

1 LONG RED CHILLI, DESEEDED AND FINELY CHOPPED

1 LEMONGRASS STALK, BRUISED AND FINELY CHOPPED

1 LIME, JUICED AND RIND JULIENNED

2 TEASPOONS FISH SAUCE

In a serving bowl combine the basil, mint, coriander and spring onions. Set aside.

Heat oil in a large frypan or wok, and lightly cook the fish for about 2 minutes till just golden brown. Transfer to a plate.

Add garlic, ginger, chilli and lemongrass to pan and cook for 2 minutes. Return the fish, lime juice and rind and fish sauce to pan. Stir-fry until heated through. Remove from the heat and add to the bowl of herbs. Stir through and serve.

TIP: If you are not into basil, mint and coriander use some rocket or baby spinach, or play around with a mix of greens to suit.

Serves 6

Warm Balsamic Fish Salad

Preheat the oven to 200°C. Line a baking tray with baking paper.

Whisk together oil, vinegar, salt and pepper in a shallow dish. Set aside half the marinade in a separate dish. Add the fish to the marinade, cover and refrigerate.

Place the pumpkin onto the baking tray. Spray with oil, season with salt and pepper to taste and roast for 20 minutes then turn. Add the zucchini and return to the oven for a further 15 minutes. Transfer to a large bowl and set aside.

Spray the asparagus with oil and season. In a large frypan (or on a barbecue grill) fry the asparagus and onion for 3 to 4 minutes over a medium heat. Add to the bowl with the pumpkin and zucchini then add the rocket and feta and toss to combine. Place salad on serving plates.

Take the fish from the refrigerator and in the same frypan cook for 2 to 3 minutes on both sides, or until cooked through. Top the salad with the fish and drizzle with reserved marinade.

Serves 4

1 TABLESPOON OLIVE OIL

1 TABLESPOON BALSAMIC VINEGAR

SALT AND PEPPER, TO TASTE

600G FISH CUT INTO THICK STRIPS

300G BUTTERNUT PUMPKIN, PEELED AND CUBED

SPRAY OLIVE OIL

2 ZUCCHINIS, CUBED

1 BUNCH ASPARAGUS, CUT INTO THIRDS

1 LARGE RED ONION, CUT INTO SMALL WEDGES

60G BABY ROCKET

35G FETA CHEESE, CRUMBLED

Prawn Noodle Salad

500G RICE NOODLES

100G SNOW PEAS

750G PRAWNS, HEADS AND
  SHELLS REMOVED, TAILS
  LEFT ON

2 LEBANESE CUCUMBERS,
  CUT IN HALF, DESEEDED AND
  FINELY SLICED

4 SPRING ONIONS, FINELY
  SLICED

½ CUP SNOW PEA SPROUTS

½ CUP CORIANDER LEAVES

½ CUP MINT LEAVES

½ LONG RED CHILLI,
  DESEEDED AND FINELY
  SLICED

DRESSING

½ CUP COCONUT MILK OR
  COCONUT CREAM

1/3 CUP SWEET CHILLI SAUCE

1 TABLESPOON FISH SAUCE

1 LIME, JUICED

Put noodles and snow peas in two separate heat-proof bowls and cover with boiling water. Leave for about 3 minutes, drain and run under cold water. Slice the snow peas lengthways.

In a serving bowl, combine the noodles, snow peas, prawns, cucumber, spring onions, snow pea sprouts, coriander, mint and chilli. In another bowl combine dressing ingredients. Pour dressing over the prawn noodle salad and toss to combine.

TIP: We also love this one with fish instead of the prawns. Just pre-grill the fish on the barbecue, break up and add to or in place of the prawns!

Serves 4

Seasoned Fish Salad

Combine the sour cream and seasoning and spread over the fish. Line a baking tray with baking paper. Place the fish on the tray and grill for 5 minutes each side or until the fish is cooked through.

Whisk together the oil, vinegar, sugar, garlic powder and salt and pepper. Place the avocado, capsicum, red onion and lettuce in a bowl. Add the dressing and toss to combine. Divide the salad between serving plates, top with the fish and sprinkle with pine nuts.

TIP: You can replace red wine vinegar with any vinegar you have on hand.

Serves 4

¼ CUP SOUR CREAM
2 TEASPOONS SEASONING OF YOUR CHOICE (WE LOVE CAJUN, MOROCCAN OR SEASON ALL)
4 FILLETS FISH
¼ CUP OLIVE OIL
2 TABLESPOONS RED WINE VINEGAR
1 TEASPOON BROWN SUGAR
¼ TEASPOON GARLIC POWDER
SALT AND PEPPER
1 AVOCADO, SLICED
1 RED CAPSICUM, FINELY SLICED
½ RED ONION, CUT INTO SMALL WEDGES
200G MIXED LETTUCE
¼ CUP TOASTED PINE NUTS

Satay Fish Salad

500G FISH, CUT INTO SMALL
FILLETS OR STRIPS
2 BUNCHES ASPARAGUS,
TRIMMED AND CUT INTO
THIRDS
120G BABY SPINACH
1 LARGE CARROT, JULIENNED
4 GREEN ONIONS, THINLY
SLICED
1 TABLESPOON TOASTED
SESAME SEEDS OR PINE NUTS

SATAY DRESSING

2 TABLESPOONS GINGER,
GRATED
½ CUP COCONUT MILK
½ CUP PEANUT BUTTER
1/3 CUP SOY SAUCE
1/3 CUP LEMON JUICE
SALT AND PEPPER, TO SEASON

In a frypan or on the barbecue, fry or grill your fish until just cooked. Let it cool.

Put asparagus in a bowl and cover with boiling water. Leave for 3 minutes then drain and run under cold water.

In a bowl, combine the spinach, carrot, onions and asparagus. Make the dressing by combining all ingredients and mixing well with a fork. Add the dressing to the salad and toss to combine. Divide between 4 serving plates and top with the fish and sesame seeds to serve.

Serves 4

Lemon Chilli Calamari Salad

Combine garlic, chilli, lemon zest and juice and 1 tablespoon of oil. Mix well. Pour over the calamari, cover and refrigerate for 15 minutes to marinate.

Combine cucumbers, coriander, rocket and onion. Mix extra lemon juice and remaining oil together, season with salt and pepper and toss through salad.

Grill calamari on a hotplate or barbecue for 1 to 2 minutes. Add to the salad and toss to combine.

TIP: Rather than rings of calamari try cutting the calamari tubes into 5cm squares and score (don't cut through) the inside with crisscross lines then cook as above.

Serves 4

4 CLOVES GARLIC, CRUSHED
1 LONG RED CHILLI, DESEEDED AND FINELY CHOPPED
1 LEMON, ZESTED AND JUICED
2 TABLESPOONS OLIVE OIL
750G CALAMARI (ABOUT 6 TUBES), CUT INTO RINGS
2 LEBANESE CUCUMBERS, HALVED LENGTHWAYS AND THINLY SLICED
1 BUNCH CORIANDER, FINELY CHOPPED
100G ROCKET
1 SMALL RED ONION
1 EXTRA LEMON, JUICED
SALT AND PEPPER TO TASTE

Smoked Fish Salad

800G CHAT POTATOES
2 TABLESPOONS CRÈME
  FRAICHE
1 LEMON, ZESTED AND JUICED
1 RED ONION, THINLY SLICED
¼ CUP BABY CAPERS,
  DRAINED
1 SMALL BUNCH FLAT LEAF
  PARSLEY, ROUGHLY CHOPPED
SALT AND PEPPER, TO TASTE
300G SMOKED FISH
PARSLEY, TO GARNISH

Boil potatoes in a large saucepan until tender. Allow to cool.

Mix crème fraiche with lemon zest and juice then add to the potatoes with the onions and capers. Season with salt and pepper and mix together gently. Top with flaked smoked fish and garnish with parsley.

NOTE: See smoked fish on page 183.

Serves 4

Fish Kebabs

Thread fish cubes onto skewers. Alternate with bay leaves allowing 2 leaves per skewer. Combine all marinade ingredients. Place kebabs in a baking dish and cover with marinade. Refrigerate, turning occasionally, for 15 minutes.

Cook on the barbecue or grill for approximately 10 to 15 minutes depending on the type of fish you use, until fish is cooked.

TIP: Replace the bay leaves with Kaffir lime leaves to add a different 'zing' to the dish.

Serves 4

800G FISH, CUBED
BAMBOO SKEWERS (PRE-
  SOAKED IN WATER)
16 BAY LEAVES

MARINADE
2 CLOVES GARLIC, FINELY
  CHOPPED
1 SMALL RED CHILLI, FINELY
  CHOPPED
PINCH SEA SALT
½ LEMON, JUICED
1 CUP OLIVE OIL

Calamari with a Honey Soy Dipping Sauce

LIGHT BITES

DIPPING SAUCE
1/3 CUP HONEY
2 TABLESPOONS SOY SAUCE
2 TABLESPOONS SWEET
 CHILLI SAUCE
1 LIME, JUICED

750G CALAMARI, CUT INTO
 RINGS
½ CUP RICE FLOUR
VEGETABLE OIL FOR DEEP-
 FRYING
SEA SALT
½ CUP PARSLEY, FINELY
 CHOPPED

Mix together the honey, soy, sweet chilli sauce and lime juice. Coat the calamari rings in rice flour.

Fill a large saucepan with oil to about 1/3 full. When oil is hot, cook the calamari in batches, for about 1 minute each batch until lightly golden. Let drain on absorbent paper.

Sprinkle with sea salt and toss with parsley. Serve on platter with dipping sauce on the side.

Serves 4

Teriyaki Fish

Slice the fish fillets into thin strips and coat in cornflour. Dip in egg and coat in the rice flour. Place on baking tray lined with baking paper. Rest in the fridge for 20-30 minutes.

Combine all the sauce ingredients in small saucepan and cook, stirring until well combined and heated through.

Heat the oil in a frypan. When hot, cook the fish in batches till golden brown and cooked through. Serve on a platter with lettuce, cucumber and sauce.

To eat, take a lettuce cup, add a piece of fish and cucumber, drizzle with the sauce, roll up and enjoy.

Serves 4

4 FILLETS FISH
¼ CUP CORNFLOUR
2 EGGS, LIGHTLY BEATEN
2 CUPS RICE FLOUR (OR YOU
  COULD USE BREADCRUMBS)
OIL, ENOUGH TO SHALLOW
  FRY
I HEAD LETTUCE, BROKEN UP
  TO MAKE LETTUCE CUPS
I CUCUMBER, SLICED INTO
  STICKS

TERIYAKI SAUCE
½ CUP TERIYAKI SAUCE
2 TABLESPOONS SOY SAUCE
2 TABLESPOONS HONEY
2 CLOVES GARLIC, CRUSHED
2 TEASPOONS GINGER,
  GRATED

Oysters Kilpatrick

This is a pretty standard recipe, but one we use whenever we are away with beautiful local oysters available to us.

1 DOZEN OYSTERS, SHUCKED
100G DICED BACON
¼ CUP TOMATO SAUCE
¼ CUP WORCESTERSHIRE
   SAUCE
1 LEMON, CUT INTO WEDGES

Line a baking tray with foil. Scrunch a second, larger sheet of foil and place it on top of the first sheet. This keeps the oysters upright and in place rather than using salt.

Arrange oysters on the foil. Sprinkle with bacon. Combine tomato sauce and Worcestershire sauce and divide over oysters. Grill until the bacon is cooked, about 5 to 10 minutes. Serve with lemon wedges.

Grilled Mussels

Each sauce variation is enough for approximately a dozen mussels.

Scrub, clean and de-beard the mussels. Using a knife, unhinge and remove the top part of the shell. Scrunch up a long length of foil to help hold the mussels upright as they cook and lay it over a baking tray. Place the mussels on the foil. Top each mussel with your chosen sauce variation below. Drizzle with oil. Cook for 3 minutes (mussels are cooked when opaque) under a hot grill.

Variation 1

The Gus

1 CLOVE GARLIC, CRUSHED

2 TABLESPOONS WORCESTERSHIRE SAUCE

½ LEMON, JUICED

SALT AND PEPPER, TO SEASON

Combine all ingredients and spoon over mussels.

Variation 2

Teriyaki

2 TABLESPOONS TERIYAKI SAUCE

1 TABLESPOON PEANUT OIL

3 DROPS SESAME OIL

2CM PIECE GINGER, FINELY GRATED

1 SPRING ONION/SHALLOT, FINELY CHOPPED

Combine the sauce, oils and ginger. Spoon over mussels and then garnish with spring onion.

Variation 3

Italian

2 SLICES PROSCIUTTO, FINELY SLICED

2 TABLESPOONS BALSAMIC VINEGAR

2 TEASPOONS OLIVE OIL

CRACKED BLACK PEPPER, TO SEASON

Top the mussels with the prosciutto. Combine vinegar and oil and spoon over the mussels. Season with pepper.

Variation 4

Sweet Balsamic

½ CUP BALSAMIC VINEGAR

1 TABLESPOON HONEY

1 TABLESPOON OLIVE OIL

Combine and spoon over mussels.

Variation 5

Thai

2 TABLESPOONS SWEET CHILLI SAUCE

½ LIME, JUICED

1 GENEROUS TABLESPOON CORIANDER, FINELY
 CHOPPED

Combine and spoon over mussels.

Variation 6

Chilli Lime

1 TABLESPOON LIME JUICE

2 TEASPOONS PEANUT OIL

1½ TEASPOONS BROWN SUGAR

1½ TEASPOONS FISH SAUCE

½ RED CHILLI, FINELY CHOPPED

Combine and spoon over mussels.

Variation 7

Curry

1 TEASPOON CURRY POWDER
2 TABLESPOONS WHITE WINE
2 TABLESPOONS COCONUT MILK
1 CLOVE GARLIC, CRUSHED
1 TABLESPOON CORIANDER, FINELY CHOPPED

Combine and spoon over mussels.

Variation 8

Chutney cream

1 TABLESPOON WORCESTERSHIRE SAUCE
1/3 CUP CHUTNEY
1 TABLESPOON CREAM
½ TEASPOON CAYENNE PEPPER
SALT, TO TASTE

Combine and spoon over mussels.

Variation 9

French

¼ CUP WHITE WINE VINEGAR
4 FRENCH SHALLOTS, FINELY CHOPPED
1 TABLESPOON CHERVIL, CHOPPED (THIS IS QUITE
 HARD TO FIND, I USE DILL WHEN I CAN'T GET IT)

Combine and spoon over mussels.

SEAFOOD PASTA

Spaghetti with Coriander, Lime and Fish

500G SPAGHETTI

250G FROZEN PEAS

OLIVE OIL SPRAY

400G FISH, CHOPPED INTO
 SMALL PIECES

1 CUP THICKENED CREAM

2 TEASPOONS BROWN SUGAR

2 LIMES, ZESTED AND JUICED

2 GARLIC CLOVES, CRUSHED

1 BUNCH OF CORIANDER,
 CHOPPED

½ RED ONION, FINELY SLICED

SALT AND PEPPER

LIME WEDGES AND EXTRA
 CORIANDER TO SERVE

Cook pasta in a large saucepan, as per packet instructions. Add the peas to the pasta in the last 4 to 5 minutes of cooking.

Spray a large frypan with light olive oil, add the fish and cook for 3 minutes (the time will obviously depend on the size of your pieces of fish). Drain the pasta and peas and add to the frypan. Add the cream, sugar, lime zest and juice, garlic, coriander and onion. Toss over a low heat until well combined. Season with salt and pepper. Serve immediately with lime wedges and extra coriander.

Serves 4

Fish Pasta with Lemon and Fennel

Cook pasta as per packet instructions. Drain well. Heat the first amount of oil in a large frypan, add fish and cook for 3 minutes then remove from the pan. Reheat the pan to a medium heat and add the extra oil. Add garlic and chilli and cook, stirring, for 1 minute or until fragrant. Reduce heat to low. Break the fish up with your fingers and return to the pan. Add the pasta, fennel and lemon rind and toss to combine and drizzle over the lemon juice. Serve immediately.

Serves 4

300G PASTA (FETTUCCINE OR SPAGHETTI ARE GOOD)

1 TABLESPOON OLIVE OIL

400G FISH, CUT INTO SMALL PIECES

¼ CUP EXTRA OLIVE OIL

3 CLOVES GARLIC, FINELY SLICED

1 LONG RED CHILLI, DESEEDED AND FINELY SLICED

1 FENNEL BULB, FINELY SLICED

1 LEMON, ZESTED AND JUICED

Fish Pasta with Basil and Mint

400G PASTA (YOUR CHOICE)
1 TABLESPOON OLIVE OIL
400G FISH, CUT INTO SMALL
 PIECES
500G TOMATO PASTA SAUCE
¼ CUP CREAM
100G SPINACH LEAVES
¼ CUP MINT LEAVES,
 SHREDDED
2 CUPS BASIL LEAVES
SALT AND PEPPER, TO TASTE
SHAVED PARMESAN CHEESE,
 TO SERVE

Cook pasta in a large saucepan as per packet instructions. Drain well. Heat oil in a large frypan and cook fish over high heat for 2 minutes. Reduce to medium to high heat and add pasta, pasta sauce, cream, spinach, mint and basil. Cook for about 2 minutes, stirring until spinach starts to wilt. Season with salt and pepper.

Serve immediately topped with Parmesan.

Serves 4

Kingfish Spaghetti

This is my take on Spaghetti Marinara. My kids won't eat shellfish of any kind at the moment, so I leave them out. If guests are coming and I am making it, in go the prawns and mussels!

Cook the spaghetti until tender, as per packet directions. Drain.

Heat oil in a large saucepan or frypan over a medium to high heat.

Add onion and garlic and cook for 3 minutes until softened. Add the tomatoes, wine, lemon rind and sugar. Stir to combine and season with salt and pepper. Bring to the boil, then reduce the heat and simmer for 10 minutes. Add the seafood (fish and/or prawns and mussels meat if using them). Cover the pan and leave to simmer for a few minutes. Stir through the parsley and basil. Pour sauce over pasta and top with Parmesan cheese.

TIP: You can also add or substitute calamari or scallops or any other seafood. If you are cooking with just the fish, use 1kg.

Serves 4

500G SPAGHETTI (OR A PASTA OF YOUR CHOICE)
2 TABLESPOONS OLIVE OIL
1 ONION, FINELY CHOPPED
3 CLOVES GARLIC, FINELY CHOPPED
800G CANNED DICED TOMATOES
½ CUP WHITE WINE
1 LEMON, RIND GRATED
SALT AND PEPPER, TO TASTE
1 LEVEL TABLESPOON CASTER SUGAR
500G (OR 2 FILLETS) KINGFISH (OR YOUR FAVOURITE FISH)
500G PRAWNS, HEADS AND SHELLS REMOVED, TAILS LEFT ON (OPTIONAL)
1 DOZEN MUSSELS, COOKED UNTIL THEY OPEN
HANDFUL PARSLEY, FINELY CHOPPED (OPTIONAL)
HANDFUL BASIL, FINELY CHOPPED
PARMESAN CHEESE, TO SERVE

Roasted Tomato, Thyme and Fish Pasta

Preheat oven to 180°C. On a baking tray lined with baking paper, lay out the tomatoes. Spray with olive oil and sprinkle with Tuscan seasoning. Put in the oven and cook for approximately 15 minutes. Cook pasta in a large saucepan as per packet instructions and drain well.

Heat oil in a large frypan. Add fish and garlic and cook for 2 minutes then reduce to medium to high heat, add pasta, diced tomatoes and thyme. Toss to combine, add roast tomatoes, season with salt and pepper and serve immediately.

NOTE: We always keep Tuscan seasoning on hand, and also take it away with us. Our alltime favourite way to do fish is with Tuscan seasoning and a little olive oil and grilled on the barbecue. Simple, quick and really delish!

Serves 4

8 ROMA TOMATOES, HALVED
TUSCAN SEASONING
(AVAILABLE IN THE
SPICE SECTION OF YOUR
SUPERMARKET)
400G FETTUCCINE
1 TABLESPOON OLIVE OIL
400G FISH, CUT INTO SMALL
PIECES
2 CLOVES GARLIC, FINELY
SLICED
400ML TINNED DICED
TOMATOES
1/3 CUP FRESH THYME,
CHOPPED
SALT AND PEPPER, TO TASTE

Fish Cannelloni

To make the béchamel sauce, melt the butter in a small saucepan over a medium heat. Add the flour and cook, stirring, for one minute. Remove from the heat and gradually whisk in the milk. Put back on the heat and cook, whisking constantly, until sauce thickens. Set aside.

Preheat oven to 200°C. Combine the minced fish, ricotta, basil and nutmeg in a bowl. Season with salt and pepper. Taking one cannelloni shell at a time, stuff with the mince mix. Set aside.

Heat the oil in a saucepan over medium heat. Add the onion and garlic and cook for 5 minutes or until softened. Add the passata and water. Bring to the boil. Set aside about 1 cup of the tomato sauce.

Spread the remaining sauce over the base of a baking dish. Place the cannelloni rolls in rows over the sauce.

Pour the reserved cup of sauce over the cannelloni, and top with the béchamel sauce. Combine the breadcrumbs, Parmesan and pine nuts and sprinkle over the top. Bake in oven for about 30 minutes. Cannelloni are ready when they are golden. Garnish with parsley and serve.

Serves 4

PASTAS

BECHAMEL SAUCE
20G BUTTER
2 TABLESPOONS PLAIN FLOUR
1 CUP MILK

CANNELLONI FILLING
400G FISH, MINCED
400G RICOTTA
1 BUNCH BASIL LEAVES, FINELY CHOPPED
½ TEASPOON GROUND NUTMEG
SALT AND PEPPER, TO TASTE
1 X 200G PACKET CANNELLONI PASTA

TOMATO SAUCE
1 TABLESPOON OLIVE OIL
1 BROWN ONION, FINELY CHOPPED
2 GARLIC CLOVES, CRUSHED
700G PASSATA SAUCE
¾ CUP WATER

BREADCRUMB TOPPING
¼ CUP BREADCRUMBS
¼ CUP SHAVED PARMESAN
¼ CUP PINE NUTS
PARSLEY, TO GARNISH

Gnocchi with Fish in a Sage, Caper and Walnut Butter

PASTAS

500G GNOCCHI

100G BUTTER, CHOPPED

400G FISH FILLETS, CHOPPED
 INTO SMALL PIECES

½ CUP SAGE LEAVES
 (SMALLER ONES)

2 TEASPOONS CAPERS,
 CHOPPED

¼ CUP WALNUTS, CHOPPED

½ TEASPOON GROUND
 NUTMEG

1 TABLESPOON CHIVES,
 FINELY CHOPPED

PEPPER, TO TASTE

Cook gnocchi to packet directions and drain. Meanwhile, melt butter over a medium heat in a large frypan, cook for 4 minutes or until butter is just golden and is frothy. Add the fish, sage, capers and walnuts and cook over a high heat for 2 to 3 minutes. Remove from the heat and stir in the nutmeg. Add gnocchi to the pan and return heat to medium and toss through for 2 minutes. Sprinkle in the chives and season with pepper.

TIP: An alternative way to present this dish is to remove fish from the pan, add the gnocchi to the pan, tossing it through. Serve the gnocchi as a side to the fish (as pictured).

Serves 4

Fish Stew

Heat oil in a large saucepan over a medium heat, add bacon, onion, leek, chilli and garlic and cook for 3 minutes. Add the tomatoes and mushrooms and cook for a further 3 minutes. Stir in the bay leaves, cloves, cinnamon stick (if you are adding it), stock and wine. Bring to the boil, then reduce heat and simmer for 10 minutes.

Stir through the fish, mussels and prawns. Cover and simmer until the mussels open. Stir in pasta, basil and parsley. Season with sea salt and pepper to taste.

Serve in a large dish, garnished with some extra parsley and lots of crusty bread.

Serves 4

2 TABLESPOONS OIL

4 RINDLESS BACON RASHERS, CHOPPED

1 ONION, CHOPPED

1 LEEK, SLICED

½ LONG RED CHILLI, FINELY SLICED

2 GARLIC CLOVES, CRUSHED

250G MINI ROMA TOMATOES, HALVED

100G MUSHROOMS, QUARTERED

4 BAY LEAVES

6 CLOVES

1 CINNAMON STICK (OPTIONAL)

2 CUPS STOCK (FISH OR CHICKEN)

200ML DRY WHITE WINE

2 FISH FILLETS, CUT INTO SMALL PIECES

½ KG MUSSELS, CLEANED AND DE-BEARDED

1 DOZEN PRAWNS, HEADS AND SHELLS REMOVED, TAILS LEFT ON

200G SMALL PASTA (I USE DITALINI OR RISSONI), PRE-COOKED

¼ CUP BASIL LEAVES, ROUGHLY CHOPPED

¼ CUP CONTINENTAL PARSLEY, ROUGHLY CHOPPED

SEA SALT

GROUND BLACK PEPPER

EXTRA PARSLEY TO GARNISH

Smoked Fish Spaghetti

500G SPAGHETTI
1 TABLESPOON OLIVE OIL
1 BABY FENNEL BULB, FINELY
  SLICED
3 GARLIC CLOVES, CRUSHED.
1 CAPSICUM, FINELY CHOPPED
1 ZUCCHINI, FINELY CHOPPED
250ML CREAM
1 TABLESPOON DIJON
  MUSTARD
SALT AND PEPPER
400-500G SMOKED FISH,
  FLAKED
4 SPRING ONIONS, FINELY
  SLICED
½ LEMON, JUICED
1/3 CUP DILL, CHOPPED
EXTRA DILL TO GARNISH

Cook spaghetti in a large saucepan, as per packet instructions. While the pasta is cooking, heat oil in large frypan over a medium-heat.

Add fennel and garlic and cook for 4 to 5 minutes. Add capsicum and zucchini and cook for a further minute. Reduce heat to medium to low. Mix cream and mustard together, season and add to the pan with the smoked fish, spring onions, lemon juice and dill. Cook for about 4 minutes until heated through.

Drain the pasta and return to saucepan. Add smoked fish mix to the pasta and toss over a low heat. Serve in a large bowl, topped with extra dill.

Serves 4

WEEKNIGHTERS

Tom's Fish Bake

My six-year-old son Tom has been fascinated with my collection of recipes, and has hounded me to help him write one for kids. One night I was trying to decide what to cook for dinner when Tom decided that he wanted 'chick-o-lata' (I was thinking 'what?'). I told him that I only had fish. 'That's okay Mum,' he replied, 'we can make fish-o-lata.' Naturally I said okay! He began pulling ingredients out of the fridge and with a lot of help from me he devised the following recipe. We all loved it and Tom is as proud as punch!

2 TOMATOES, EITHER SLICED
OR CUT INTO THIN WEDGES
2 ZUCCHINIS, SLICED
2 TABLESPOONS SUN-DRIED
TOMATOES, ROUGHLY CHOPPED
1 TABLESPOON BUTTER
2 TABLESPOONS OLIVE OIL
1 BROWN ONION, FINELY SLICED
4 RINDLESS BACON RASHERS,
DICED
1 SMALL RED CHILLI, DESEEDED
AND THINLY SLICED
(OPTIONAL)
3 CLOVES GARLIC, ROUGHLY
CHOPPED
4-6 FISH FILLETS (TOM'S
FAVOURITE IS KINGFISH)
SPRAY OLIVE OIL
2 SPRING ONIONS, SLICED
1 CARROT, JULIENNED
½ HANDFUL BASIL LEAVES
½ HANDFUL MINT LEAVES
¼ CUP CHICKEN OR VEGETABLE
STOCK (OR DRY WHITE WINE)
SEA SALT
CRACKED PEPPER

Preheat oven 220°C. Combine tomatoes, zucchini and sun-dried tomatoes in a bowl and set aside. Heat butter and oil in small frypan. Add onion, bacon, chilli, and garlic. Reduce heat to medium and cook for 5 minutes then set aside on a plate.

In the same frypan sear the fish fillets on both sides over a high heat. In a baking dish, lightly sprayed with olive oil, lay the seared kingfish fillets. Top with tomato/zucchini mix, spring onions, carrot, basil, mint and the onion/bacon mix. Pour stock over and season with salt and pepper.

Cook in the oven for about 15 to 20 minutes.

Serves 4-6

I hope you like
my Fish Bake.
Thomas McGloshan

Basic Fish Pie

This can be made in the ramekins as suggested or made in a baking dish as one large family pie.

2 TABLESPOONS OLIVE OIL

4 ONIONS, THINLY SLICED

2 CLOVES GARLIC, CRUSHED

1 TEASPOON VEGETABLE
 STOCK POWDER (I USE
 VEGETA)

3 TABLESPOONS FLOUR

1½ CUPS FISH STOCK

2 CUPS MILK

1 CUP CREAM

1KG FISH, CUBED

SALT AND PEPPER, TO SEASON

2 SHEETS PUFF PASTRY

1 EGG, LIGHTLY BEATEN

Heat oven to 220°C. Heat oil in a large saucepan over medium-high heat, then add onion and garlic, stirring until softened. Add vegetable stock and stir through, cooking for a further minute. Add flour and mix well. Pour in fish stock, milk and cream, stir and simmer gently over medium to low heat for about 5 minutes and then add fish. Simmer for a further 5 to 10 minutes until sauce thickens. Season to taste.

Divide mixture evenly between ramekins. Cut puff pastry into rounds slightly larger than the ramekins. Brush egg around edge of pastry, place on top of the ramekins, brushing more egg over the top of the pie. Bake in the oven for 20 minutes or until golden brown.

TIP: Take this basic fish pie recipe and make it your own by adding flavours you have on hand or love, as I have done with the following 3 recipes.

Serves 6

Fennel and Fish Pie

This can be made in the ramekins as suggested or made in a baking dish as one large family pie.

Preheat oven to 220°C. Heat oil in a large saucepan over a medium-high heat. Add fennel and garlic, stirring until softened. Add vegetable stock, stir through and cook for a further minute. Add flour and mix well. Pour in fish stock, milk and cream. Stir, then simmer gently over medium to low heat for approximately 5 minutes and then add fish. Simmer for a further 5 to 10 minutes until sauce thickens. Add thyme and seasoning and stir through.

Divide the mixture evenly between 6 ramekins. Cut puff pastry into rounds slightly larger than the ramekins. Brush egg around the edge of the pastry and put over the ramekins. Brush more egg over the top of the pie. Bake in the oven for 20 minutes or until golden brown.

Serves 6

2 TABLESPOONS OLIVE OIL
2 FENNEL BULBS, FINELY CHOPPED
2 CLOVES GARLIC, FINELY CHOPPED
1 TEASPOON VEGETABLE STOCK POWDER (I USE VEGETA)
3 TABLESPOONS FLOUR
1½ CUPS FISH STOCK
2 CUPS MILK
1 CUP CREAM
1KG FISH, CUBED
SALT AND PEPPER, TO SEASON
¼ CUP THYME, CHOPPED
2 SHEETS PUFF PASTRY
1 EGG, LIGHTLY BEATEN

Bacon and Fish Pie

This can be made in the ramekins as suggested or made in a baking dish as one large family pie.

2 TABLESPOONS OLIVE OIL

2 ONIONS, THINLY SLICED

2 CLOVES GARLIC, CRUSHED

2 STALKS CELERY, FINELY SLICED

2 BACON RASHERS, ROUGHLY CHOPPED

1 TEASPOON VEGETABLE STOCK POWDER (I USE VEGETA)

3 TABLESPOONS FLOUR

1½ CUPS FISH STOCK

2 CUPS MILK

1 CUP CREAM

1KG FISH, CUBED

SALT AND PEPPER, TO SEASON

¼ CUP PARSLEY

2 SHEETS PUFF PASTRY

1 EGG, LIGHTLY BEATEN

Preheat oven to 220°C. Heat oil a large saucepan over medium to high heat, then add onion, garlic, celery and bacon and stir until softened. Add vegetable stock and stir through, cooking for a further minute. Add flour and mix well. Pour in fish stock, milk and cream and stir. Simmer gently over medium-low heat for 5 minutes then add fish. Simmer for a further 5 to 10 minutes until sauce thickens. Remove from heat and add parsley.

Divide mixture evenly between 6 ramekins. Cut puff pastry into rounds slightly larger than the ramekins. Brush egg around edge of pastry, place on top of the ramekins, brushing more egg over the top of the pie. Bake in the oven for 20 minutes or until golden brown.

Potato/cheese topping variation

Boil 4 large potatoes until soft. Mash with salt and pepper to season, add 1 tablespoon butter and a little milk or cream.

Add handful grated cheese. When pie mixture is in ramekins, spoon potato mash on top, add dollop of butter and sprinkle over grated cheese. The cooking time remains the same.

Leek and Fish Pie

This can be made in the ramekins as suggested or made in a baking dish as one large family pie.

2 TABLESPOONS OLIVE OIL

2 LEEKS, FINELY SLICED

2 CLOVES GARLIC, FINELY CHOPPED

1 TEASPOON VEGETABLE STOCK POWDER (I USE VEGETA)

1 LEMON, ZESTED

3 TABLESPOONS FLOUR

1½ CUPS FISH STOCK

2 CUPS MILK

1 CUP CREAM

1KG FISH, CUBED

SALT AND PEPPER TO SEASON

¼ CUP CHOPPED DILL

2 SHEETS PUFF PASTRY

1 EGG, LIGHTLY BEATEN

Preheat oven to 220°C. Heat oil in a large saucepan over medium to high heat, add leeks and garlic and stir until softened. Add vegetable stock and lemon zest, cooking for a further minute. Add flour and mix well. Pour in fish stock, milk and cream and stir well. Simmer gently over medium to low heat for 5 minutes then add fish. Simmer for a further 5 to 10 minutes until sauce thickens. Add dill and stir through. Season to taste.

Divide the mixture evenly between 6 ramekins. Cut puff pastry into rounds slightly larger than the ramekins. Brush egg around the edge of the pastry and put over the ramekins. Brush more egg over the top of the pie. Bake in the oven for 20 minutes or until golden brown.

Serves 6

Basil and Mint Crumbed Fish

Preheat oven to 180°C.

In a food processor, blend the cashews, rolled oats, basil and mint, until finely chopped. Remove to a bowl and mix in the breadcrumbs. Arrange the flour, egg and crumb mix on separate plates. Coat the fish in flour, the egg and finally in the crumb mix.

In a frypan, over a high heat, heat enough vegetable oil to fill the base of the pan to 1cm. Shallow-fry the fish for 2 minutes on each side. Transfer the fish to a wire rack over a baking tray. Bake in the oven for 10 minutes or until fish is cooked through. Cooking time will depend on the size of your fillets. Serve garnished with parsley and sprinkled with a pinch of sea salt.

Serves 4

1/3 CUP CASHEWS
¼ CUP ROLLED OATS
½ CUP BASIL LEAVES
½ CUP MINT LEAVES
1½ CUPS BREADCRUMBS
½ CUP PLAIN FLOUR
2 EGGS, LIGHTLY BEATEN
4 FISH FILLETS
VEGETABLE OIL
PARSLEY, TO GARNISH
PINCH OF SEA SALT

Oven-baked Fish Risotto

Preheat oven to 200°C.

Lay the fish, carrots, zucchini, onion and rice in a baking dish. Pour in the stock and stir to combine. Scatter the butter evenly on top. Cover the dish with foil and put in the oven for 30-40 minutes or until the rice is tender. Stir in the cheese and basil and season.

Serves 4

400G FISH, DICED
2 CARROTS, DICED
1 ZUCCHINI, DICED
1 ONION, FINELY CHOPPED
1 CUP ARBORIO RICE
2½ CUPS CHICKEN STOCK
30G BUTTER, CHOPPED
2 TABLESPOONS PARMESAN
 CHEESE, GRATED
½ CUP BASIL LEAVES, TORN
SALT AND PEPPER, TO TASTE

Glazed Fish Loaf

GLAZE
1 TEASPOON DRY MUSTARD
1/2 CUP TOMATO SAUCE
2 TABLESPOONS BROWN
  SUGAR

LOAF
500G FISH, MINCED
2 CLOVES GARLIC, CRUSHED
1 SMALL RED CHILLI, FINELY
  CHOPPED
1/3 CUP BREADCRUMBS
1 EGG
1 TABLESPOON
  WORCESTERSHIRE SAUCE
1/3 CUP FRESH BASIL LEAVES,
  CHOPPED
1/3 CUP SUN-DRIED
  TOMATOES (WITH OIL),
  CHOPPED
2 TABLESPOONS ROASTED
  PINE NUTS, CHOPPED
½ ONION, CHOPPED
4 SLICES PROSCIUTTO

Combine glaze ingredients and set aside. Preheat oven to 220°C.

Mix all the remaining ingredients, except the prosciutto and press into a greased tin loaf (roughly 20cm x 10cm tin).

Turn upside down onto an oven tray lined with baking paper, leaving tin on. Bake in the oven for 10 minutes. Remove from oven and remove tin.

Brush with the glaze, being generous but reserving a little. Lay prosciutto over fish loaf and return to the oven for a further 10 minutes. Glaze again then bake for a further 5 to 10 minutes until prosciutto is crispy.

Serves 4

Stuffed Fish

Preheat oven to 240°C. Melt butter in frypan, add garlic, shallots and bacon and cook over medium heat for about 5 minutes. Season and add parsley, coriander and breadcrumbs. Remove from heat, mix in egg and allow to cool.

Prepare fish as below depending on whether it's a whole fish or fillets.

For whole fish:
Season inside of fish with salt and pepper. Stuff and tie together with string. Grease a baking dish with butter. Lay fish in and pour over the wine. Bake for 45 minutes (a smaller fish like whiting will only take 20 -30 minutes) – basting with wine while cooking. Remove fish to serving plate.

For fillets:
Lay fillets flat on bench, place 1 to 2 tablespoons of stuffing on one end of fish. Roll up and secure with a toothpick. Place on a greased baking dish. Sprinkle fish with Parmesan cheese and cook for 20 to 25 minutes then remove to serving plate.

Once fish is plated, pour remaining juice from baking dish in small saucepan. Add wine to saucepan and bring to the boil. Boil until wine reduces, then add crème fraiche. Reduce heat to medium and stir until thickens. Pour over fish. Garnish with parsley.

40G BUTTER
4 CLOVES GARLIC, FINELY CHOPPED
5 SHALLOTS, FINELY CHOPPED
3 RINDLESS RASHERS OF BACON, FINELY DICED
SEA SALT AND BLACK PEPPER
1/3 CUP CHOPPED PARSLEY
¼ CUP CHOPPED CORIANDER
¾ CUP BREADCRUMBS (I USE 'KRUMMIES')
1 EGG
WHOLE FISH (CLEANED AND GUTTED)
OR
4 FISH FILLETS, VERY CAREFULLY SLICED IN HALF LENGTHWAYS
1/3 CUP GRATED PARMESAN
½ CUP WHITE WINE
¾ CUP CRÈME FRAICHE
PARSLEY, TO GARNISH

Mustard Baked Tuna

2 TABLESPOONS OLIVE OIL
1 SMALL FENNEL BULB,
  FINELY CHOPPED
1 TABLESPOON GARLIC,
  MINCED
540G COCONUT MILK
2 TABLESPOONS WHOLEGRAIN
  MUSTARD
4 TUNA STEAKS
OIL SPRAY
½ ROUND BRIE (ABOUT
  100G), SLICED
¼ CUP CHIVES, FINELY
  CHOPPED
¼ CUP LEMON THYME
1 CARROT, JULIENNED
½ RED CAPSICUM, JULIENNED
½ YELLOW CAPSICUM,
  JULIENNED
2 SPRING ONIONS, JULIENNED
CONTINENTAL PARSLEY AND
  LEMON JUICE OF WEDGES TO
  SERVE

Preheat oven to 220°C. In a medium saucepan, heat olive oil over a medium-high heat. Add fennel and garlic and cook until soft. Pour in coconut milk and mustard and simmer over a low heat for 2 to 3 minutes until heated through.

Spray a baking dish with oil, lay tuna out in the dish and top each steak with brie, herbs and vegetables. Pour sauce over the top, cover with foil and bake for 10 to 15 minutes. Serve with a drizzle of lemon juice and parsley to garnish.

Serves 4

Roasted Balsamic Fish

Preheat oven to 220°C.

In a large bowl, combine mushrooms, zucchini, capsicum, parsnip, fennel, garlic, fish, vinegar, oil, dried oregano, rosemary and a good pinch of sea salt. Toss to combine all ingredients. Spoon the mixture into a roasting pan and roast for 20 to 30 minutes, stirring halfway through cooking time, until fish has cooked through.

Crumble ricotta (or feta) cheese over the dish and drizzle with a little extra oil. Season with salt and pepper.

Serves 4

250G MUSHROOMS (I LIKE SWISS BROWN)
2 ZUCCHINIS, CHOPPED
1 RED CAPSICUM, SLICED THICKLY (I LIKE BABY CAPSICUM)
1 PARSNIP, CHOPPED
1 BABY FENNEL, BULB ONLY FINELY SLICED
4 GARLIC CLOVES, THINLY SLICED
500G FISH, CHOPPED INTO LARGE CUBES
¼ CUP BALSAMIC VINEGAR
2 TABLESPOONS EXTRA VIRGIN OLIVE OIL
3 TEASPOONS DRIED OREGANO
3 SPRIGS ROSEMARY LEAVES
SEA SALT
1/3 CUP FRESH RICOTTA OR FETA CHEESE
EXTRA OLIVE OIL
SALT AND PEPPER

Fish Scallopini

4 FISH FILLETS
1 TABLESPOON OLIVE OIL
250G TOMATO PASTA SAUCE
½ CUP BASIL LEAVES,
  SHREDDED
½ CUP PITTED KALAMATA
  OLIVES
2 X 125G BALLS MOZZARELLA,
  EACH BALL SLICED THINLY
  AND PATTED DRY WITH
  ABSORBENT PAPER
4 SLICES PROSCIUTTO,
  HALVED
½ BUNCH BASIL LEAVES,
  EXTRA

Preheat grill to a high heat.

Heat oil in a frypan over a medium-high heat. Sear fish for 2 minutes each side until golden then remove from heat. Heat pasta sauce in a saucepan over a medium heat, then stir through shredded basil and olives. Pour into a baking dish and place fish in dish on top of sauce. Top with mozzarella, extra basil leaves and prosciutto.

Place under the grill for 6 to 8 minutes. Mozzarella should be bubbling by this time and prosciutto should be golden and crunchy. Serve with steamed vegetables.

Serves 4

Coconut Crumbed Fish

1/3 CUP SHREDDED COCONUT

1 CUP BREADCRUMBS

1/3 CUP PARSLEY, FINELY
   CHOPPED

2 TABLESPOONS THYME,
   FINELY CHOPPED

1 TEASPOON GARLIC
   GRANULES

4 FISH FILLETS

1 EGG WHITE, LIGHTLY
   BEATEN

OIL SPRAY

Preheat oven to 220°C. Line a baking tray with baking paper.

Combine the coconut, breadcrumbs, parsley, thyme and garlic.

Take each fish fillet and dip in egg white and then coat with the crumb mix.

Place on the baking tray, spray with oil and bake for 15 to 20 minutes until golden and cooked through.

TIP: Be brave and try substituting the flavours. Try chilli flakes instead of parsley and thyme. You may not always get it right but use the recipes only as a guide and use flavours your family like!

Macadamia Crusted Fish

Combine macadamias, basil, parsley and butter.

Heat oil in a frypan over a medium-high heat and cook fish for 3 minutes on each side. Remove from heat.

Preheat grill. Line a baking tray with baking paper and place fish on the tray. Top each fillet with the nut mix, pressing down firmly. Grill for 1 to 2 minutes until golden.

Variations

Replace with cashews or almonds in place of the macadamias. You can also add the rind of 1 lemon into the mix.

Instead of frying the fish, drizzle with a little olive oil and bake with the nut mix on top for about 12 minutes in a preheated oven at 220°C.

Serves 4

1 CUP ROASTED MACADAMIA
NUTS, FINELY CHOPPED
1 TABLESPOON BASIL LEAVES,
FINELY CHOPPED
1 TABLESPOON PARSLEY,
FINELY CHOPPED
1 TABLESPOON BUTTER,
MELTED
4 FISH FILLETS
2 TABLESPOONS OLIVE OIL

Fish in a Wine Cream Sauce

4 TABLESPOONS BUTTER
1 TABLESPOON OLIVE OIL
1 SMALL ONION, FINELY
  CHOPPED
4 FISH FILLETS
5 CLOVES OF GARLIC, FINELY
  CHOPPED
100ML WHITE WINE
300ML CREAM
FLAT LEAF PARSLEY,
  CHOPPED
SALT AND PEPPER TO SEASON

Heat butter and oil in a large frypan over a medium heat. Sauté onion for 3 minutes until softened. Add fish and garlic, increase heat marginally and cook, turning and stirring, until fish is lightly golden. Remove to a plate.

Pour wine into the pan and simmer until reduced by half. Return fish to pan and add cream. Season with salt and pepper. Simmer gently until fish is cooked through. Serve garnished with parsley and a side of your choice.

Serves 4

Fish with Honey Mustard Sauce

Heat the oil and butter in a small saucepan, add garlic and cook for 1 minute. Reduce the heat to medium, pour in the wine and cook until reduced by half. Add the rosemary and stir through.

Stir in 1 tablespoon of honey mustard, test the flavour and add more if you prefer. Remove the sauce from the heat and keep warm.

In a frypan, heat extra oil over a medium high heat, add the fish and cook for 2 to 3 minutes each side or until cooked through. Divide fillets between 4 dinner plates and pour honey mustard sauce over. Serve with steamed vegetables.

Serves 4

2 TABLESPOONS OLIVE OIL
30G BUTTER
2 CLOVES GARLIC, CRUSHED
1 CUP DRY WHITE WINE
1 SPRIG ROSEMARY LEAVES, FINELY CHOPPED
1-2 TABLESPOONS HONEY MUSTARD
2 TABLESPOONS EXTRA OLIVE OIL
4 FISH FILLETS

Fish Kiev

125G BUTTER, SOFTENED

2 CLOVES GARLIC, CRUSHED

I TEASPOON LEMON ZEST

I TABLESPOON FRESH CHIVES,
  CHOPPED

I TABLESPOON FRESH DILL,
  CHOPPED

I TABLESPOON FRESH
  PARSLEY, CHOPPED

4 THICK FISH FILLETS

I CUP PLAIN FLOUR
  (SEASONED WITH SALT AND
  PEPPER)

2 EGGS, LIGHTLY BEATEN

2 CUPS BREADCRUMBS

I BUNCH FRESH ASPARAGUS

EXTRA BUTTER, TO SERVE

PARSLEY, TO GARNISH

Combine butter, garlic, zest and herbs in bowl. Spoon mixture onto a sheet of plastic wrap and roll into a log shape. Freeze until firm.

Preheat oven to 180°C.

Slice up the butter roll into 12 discs. Take each fillet of fish and using sharp knife cut through middle making a pocket. Place 3 discs into each fillet. Dip the fillets in flour, then in egg and then breadcrumbs. Lay on a plate and refrigerate for 30 minutes.

Bake fish in the oven for 30 minutes until golden brown and cooked through. Place asparagus in bowl and cover in hot water for 1 to 2 minutes. Serve fish with the asparagus. Melt the extra butter mix in microwave and pour over to serve, with a sprig of parsley to garnish.

Serves 4

Fish Parcels

Fish parcels are a marvellous, quick and superbly easy way to prepare fish. Believe me, you will impress anyone! The options are limitless flavour-wise. I always come back to cooking fish in parcels if I am running short on time, as they need so little preparation.

Here are just three of our favourites. These quantities should easily make 4 parcels easily (1 fillet of fish per parcel). The flavourings could also be used on barbecue fish, on whole fish or for steamed fish.

Preheat the oven to 200°C or preheat your barbecue.

Combine all the ingredients for your chosen sauce. Break off a large square of aluminium foil and a slightly smaller piece of baking paper. Lay the baking paper on top of the foil and place a fillet on top of the baking paper. Repeat for each fillet of fish.

Divide the sauce mix between the fillets, bring the edges of the foil up to meet at the centre and fold over. Next fold the ends in towards the centre, sealing the fish into a parcel.

If you are cooking the parcels in the oven, place them on a baking tray and cook for about 15 minutes or until cooked. I take a peek and test with a fork, if it flakes easily it's done.

If cooking on the barbecue, put the parcels on the grill plate and cook for about 3 to 4 minutes each side. Once again take a peek and test the fish to determine if it's cooked.

Makes 4 parcels

SAUCE #1

2 LIMES, JUICED

¼ CUP OLIVE OIL

2 TEASPOONS POWDERED VEGETABLE STOCK (I USE VEGETA)

1 CLOVE GARLIC, CRUSHED

2 SPRING ONIONS, FINELY SLICED

PEPPER, TO TASTE

SAUCE #2

¼ CUP TERIYAKI SAUCE

1 TABLESPOON SOY SAUCE

1 TABLESPOON OIL

1 TEASPOON GINGER, GRATED

1 SMALL CHILLI, FINELY CHOPPED

1 CLOVE GARLIC, CRUSHED

SAUCE #3 (PICTURED)

2 LONG RED CHILLIES, DESEEDED AND FINELY CHOPPED

2 GARLIC CLOVES, CRUSHED

1 LIME, ZESTED AND JUICED

1 CUP CORIANDER LEAVES, CHOPPED

2 TABLESPOONS FISH SAUCE

¼ CUP COCONUT CREAM

Fish and Bacon Wraps

I use tuna or kingfish for this dish. It is great with both.

STUFFING

1 CLOVE GARLIC

4 TABLESPOONS PARSLEY

4 CUPS (250G) SAVOURY
  CRACKERS

2/3 CUP MACADAMIA NUTS

4 SPRING ONIONS (SHALLOTS)

1 ONION

1 TEASPOON DRIED OREGANO

1 TEASPOON SALT
  (OPTIONAL)

½ CUP MELTED BUTTER

2 TABLESPOONS WHITE WINE

6 RASHERS BACON, CUT IN
  HALF

6 FILLETS FISH (SLICED IN
  HALF TO THIN THEM OUT
  TO ABOUT THE LENGTH AND
  WIDTH OF A RASHER OF
  BACON

OLIVE OIL SPRAY

Make the stuffing: Combine all the stuffing ingredients using a food processor. Mix with butter and wine. Preheat oven to 220°C. Lay out a rasher of bacon. Place a thin fillet of fish on top of bacon. Take about a tablespoon of stuffing and, using your hands, shape into an oblong shape. Roll up with bacon and fish, and secure with a toothpick. Complete all rolls.

Put all the rolls (there should be 6) on a tray lined with baking paper and spray with olive oil. Bake in oven for 15-20 minutes. If bacon is not browned turn up the heat to 240°C for 5 minutes or so.

Serve atop either steam asparagus or green beans and top with optional balsamic butter sauce, see below.

TIP: The stuffing makes this recipe and that is due to the savoury crackers. I use Ritz or Savoy but you can use any available. You can also use this stuffing in a whole fish, baked in the oven.

OPTIONAL BALSAMIC BUTTER SAUCE

50G BUTTER

1 TABLESPOON PEANUT OIL

1 TABLESPOON CRUSHED GARLIC

2 TABLESPOONS BALSAMIC VINEGAR

Heat the oil and butter in pan over a medium-high heat. When the butter is melted, add the garlic and balsamic vinegar. Bring to the boil, turn to a low heat and reduce the liquid to half.

Makes 6

Coconut and Lime Fish Curry

Heat oil in a large frypan or wok. Add curry paste, ginger and lemongrass. Stir-fry for 30 seconds until fragrant. Add fish and stir-fry for 2 to 3 minutes.

Add coconut cream, fish sauce, brown sugar, tomatoes and lime rind. Stir-fry for 2 to 3 minutes until tomatoes 'collapse'. Stir through the coriander and lime juice. Serve immediately on rice with lime wedges on the side.

NOTE: Grated ginger and lemongrass are optional; I originally cooked this dish without them. It works either way!

Serves 6

2 TABLESPOONS PEANUT OIL
2 TEASPOONS GREEN CURRY
 PASTE
1 TEASPOON GINGER, GRATED
1 TEASPOON LEMONGRASS*
600G FISH, CUBED (KINGFISH,
 TUNA OR MAHI MAHI
 PREFERRED)
400ML CAN COCONUT CREAM
1 TABLESPOON FISH SAUCE
2 TEASPOONS BROWN SUGAR
250G MINI ROMA TOMATOES
 (OR CHERRY TOMATOES)
1 LIME, ZESTED AND JUICED
1 BUNCH CORIANDER
LIME WEDGES AND STEAMED
JASMINE RICE, TO SERVE

*I USE A JAR OF LEMONGRASS
(FROM THE SUPERMARKET)
HERE, BUT YOU CAN USE
A 5CM STALK OF FRESH
LEMONGRASS, BRUISED AND
FINELY CHOPPED.

BARBIE, BOAT OR BEACH

Barbecue Seafood Extravaganza

We often spend fishing trips with friends, which usually means the boys come in from fishing starving, the girls have been busy (lying on the beach, shopping, getting nails done or reading a book! Don't I wish!) This is a great social meal. It is all done on the barbecue and everyone just tucks in. Choose between our two favourite marinades.

3 FISH FILLETS, CUT INTO THIRDS

1 DOZEN MUSSELS, WASHED AND DE-BEARDED

2 BLUE SWIMMER CRABS, COOKED, CUT IN HALF AND CLEANED

1 DOZEN PRAWNS, HEADS AND SHELLS REMOVED, TAILS LEFT ON

1 DOZEN SCALLOPS

2 SQUID TUBES, CLEANED AND CUT INTO RINGS

MARINADE #1

¼ CUP OLIVE OIL

330-375 ML (1 STUBBY) DARK BEER (START WITH ½ A BOTTLE AND ADD TO TASTE—I USE ALL)

1 LEMON, JUICED

5 GARLIC CLOVES, FINELY CHOPPED

5 BAY LEAVES

1 TEASPOON DRY MUSTARD

HANDFUL OF BASIL LEAVES, CHOPPED

HANDFUL OF OREGANO, CHOPPED

HANDFUL OF THYME, CHOPPED

GOOD PINCH SEA SALT

PEPPER

MARINADE #2

¼ CUP OLIVE OIL

2 LEMONS, JUICED

¼ CUP SOY SAUCE

1 LONG RED CHILLI, FINELY SLICED

5 CLOVES GARLIC, FINELY CHOPPED

3CM PIECE GINGER, FINELY CHOPPED

2 TABLESPOONS HONEY

1 BUNCH CORIANDER, CHOPPED

Combine your chosen marinade ingredients in a large container and add seafood. Marinate for 1 hour in the fridge. Barbecue all together until fish has cooked and mussels have opened. Serve in large bowl in the middle of the table.

TIP: Remember that the calamari and scallops will cook very quickly. We tend to leave these to the outer rim of the barbecue, same goes if you have precooked prawns that just need to be heated through. Cook this dish outside on a Cobb cooker (pictured).

Honey Vinaigrette Prawns

Heat lightly oiled barbecue plate and cook prawns or grill them till heated through. Place garlic, mustard, honey, vinegar, lime juice and olive oil in a saucepan. Add butter and heat until boiling. Stir through dill and pour over prawns. Serve immediately with crusty bread.

TIP: this is also wonderful with yabbies (see page 184).

Serves 4

20 PRAWNS, HEADS AND
  SHELLS REMOVED, TAILS
  LEFT ON
3 CLOVES GARLIC, CRUSHED
2 TABLESPOONS WHOLEGRAIN
  MUSTARD
¼ CUP HONEY
1 TABLESPOON BALSAMIC
  VINEGAR
¼ CUP LIME JUICE
½ CUP LIGHT OLIVE OIL
30G BUTTER
2 TABLESPOONS FRESH DILL,
  CHOPPED
CRUSTY BREAD, TO SERVE

BARBIE, BOAT OR BEACH

Garlic and Coriander Blue Swimmer Crab

1 TABLESPOON HONEY

1 TABLESPOON SOY SAUCE

1 CLOVE GARLIC, CRUSHED

2 TABLESPOONS OLIVE OIL

1 COOKED BLUE SWIMMER
   CRAB, CUT IN HALF AND
   CLEANED

¼ CUP CORIANDER, ROUGHLY
   CHOPPED

Combine honey, soy sauce, garlic and oil in a dish, then add the crab. Cover and place in the refrigerator for 1 hour to marinate.

Preheat the grill plate on the barbecue. Toss half the coriander with the crab. Cook on the barbecue for about 5 minutes, remembering you are really only heating up the crab. Serve on platter with remaining half of coriander scattered over the top.

Serves 1

Mussels in a Cream Sauce

This is one of those dishes I love to make when friends come around for a relaxed meal. So very easy to make, which allows me more time to enjoy a glass of wine with my friends.

In a large saucepan, heat cider over a high heat. Bring to the boil.

Add the shallots and onions, boil for 2 minutes then add the mussels and cover the pan. When the mussels open, remove them to a serving bowl.

Add half the crème fraiche to the saucepan. Cook, stirring, for 2 minutes over a high heat then strain the liquid into a small saucepan. Put the strained shallots and onions over the mussels.

Whisk together the remaining crème fraiche and the egg yolks. Pour into the small saucepan with the juice, season and whisk over a low heat until thick and creamy. Stir in the parsley, pour over the mussels and enjoy.

TIP: Some mussels speicies, for example New Zealand green lips, do not always open when cooked.

Serves 4

1 STUBBY (330ML) STRONGBOW SWEET CIDER
2 FRENCH SHALLOTS
3 SPRING ONIONS
1KG MUSSELS, WASHED AND DEBEARDED
250G CRÈME FRAICHE
3 EGG YOLKS
SALT AND PEPPER, TO SEASON
1 CUP PARSLEY, ROUGHLY CHOPPED

Tuna Tartare

Al loves his raw fish with soy and wasabi, so I got to playing around with flavours and ingredients for him and the boys when they come in from fishing and present me with a fresh fillet to cut up! We use tuna for this one but you can use this with any raw fish. It's good with kingfish too.

200G RAW FISH, FINELY CHOPPED

1 ROMA TOMATO, DESEEDED AND FINELY CHOPPED

1 SPRING ONION, FINELY CHOPPED

1 LIME, JUICED

½ BUNCH CORIANDER LEAVES, FINELY CHOPPED

1 TEASPOON RED CHILLI, DESEEDED AND FINELY CHOPPED

2 CUCUMBERS, CUT INTO 1CM SLICES

Combine fish, tomato, spring onion, lime juice, coriander and chilli in a bowl. Stir, cover and refrigerate for 1 hour. Using a teaspoon scoop slight indentations out of each cucumber slice to create 'cups'. Remove fish mix from fridge and drain any juice off. Use a teaspoon to divide the mixture among the cucumber 'cups' and serve.

TIP: You could also serve this on crackers or mini toasts (pictured).

VARIATION
1 MEDIUM AVOCADO, FLESH DICED
2 TABLESPOON NATURAL YOGHURT (LOW FAT IS GOOD)

Add avocado and yoghurt to the fish mix. Stir to combine, then proceed as above.

Surf 'n' Seafood

We love this recipe, but we have learned to avoid oily fish like tuna. I find it absorbs the rice flour and you do not get the crispness.

Put rice flour in a shallow bowl and coat the prawns and fish. Place seafood in refrigerator for 30 minutes. Combine basil, coriander, spring onion, chilli and snow peas in a bowl and set aside. Mix soy sauce and ginger and set aside.

Heat enough oil to coat the bottom of a deep pan to about 1cm.

Cook the fish until golden and crisp, for 2 to 4 minutes each side then drain on absorbent paper. Cook prawns until golden and crisp or about 1 minute each side then drain on absorbent paper. Pour soy and ginger over salad greens. Place fish on a platter, top with salad and then prawns. Serve with dipping bowl of Rachel's Mayonnaise (see below).

RACHEL'S MAYONNAISE
½ CUP WHOLE EGG MAYONNAISE
1 TABLESPOON SOY SAUCE
1 TEASPOON GINGER, GRATED

Combine all ingredients and mix.

1–1½ CUPS RICE FLOUR
20 KING PRAWNS, HEADS AND
  SHELLS REMOVED, TAILS
  LEFT ON
4 FISH FILLETS, CUT INTO 4
  PIECES EACH
1 BUNCH BASIL LEAVES,
  CHOPPED (YOU CAN USE
  THAI BASIL FOR COLOUR)
1 BUNCH CORIANDER LEAVES,
  CHOPPED
2 SPRING ONIONS, JULIENNED
1 LARGE CHILLI, DESEEDED
  AND JULIENNED
200G SNOW PEAS, BLANCHED
  AND JULIENNED
¼ CUP OF SOY SAUCE
1 TABLESPOON GINGER,
  GRATED
VEGETABLE OR RICE BRAN
  OIL

Honey Ginger Seafood Stack

1/3 CUP HONEY

3CM PIECE GINGER, FINELY
 CHOPPED OR GRATED

3 GARLIC CLOVES, CRUSHED

2 TABLESPOONS LIME JUICE

1 DOZEN RAW PRAWNS,
 DEVEINED, HEADS REMOVED,
 TAILS LEFT ON

1 DOZEN SCALLOPS

¼ CUP PEANUT OIL

4 FISH FILLETS

1 RED ONION, CUT INTO
 WEDGES

1 CARROT, CUT INTO MATCH
 STICKS

1 GREEN CAPSICUM, CUT INTO
 MATCH STICKS

100G SNOW PEAS

½ CUP CORIANDER LEAVES,
 CHOPPED

EXTRA CORIANDER TO
 GARNISH

Combine the honey, ginger, garlic and lime juice in a bowl. Set half aside for later. Add the prawns and scallops to the remaining marinade. Cover and marinate for 15 minutes.

In a frypan, heat 1 tablespoon of the oil, add fish and cook for 2 to 3 minutes each side until cooked. Remove to a plate and keep warm.

In the same pan heat another tablespoon of oil, add the prawns and scallops and cook for 2 to 3 minutes. Remove to a plate and keep warm. Heat remaining oil and add onion, carrot and capsicum. Stir-fry for 2 minutes. Add the snow peas and stirfry for a further minute. Remove from the heat and toss the coriander through. Divide vegetables among four plates. Top with the fish, prawns and scallops. Drizzle with reserved marinade and garnish with extra coriander.

Serves 4

BATTERED FISH

If you can handle the oil, deep-frying is a great way to enjoy seafood. Heat the oil so it covers the bottom of the pan for at least 10 cm until it is nearly smoking. Leave the fish in the oil for about four minutes, depending on the size of your fillet. A sieve is handy to place over the pan to cut oil spatter, or a deep frying appliance is also great. To test if the oil is ready, use a small piece of bread. The oil is hot enough if the bread sizzles. After you make the batter, leave it to sit for about an hour to rest before using.

Plain

1 CUP PLAIN FLOUR
½ TEASPOON SALT
1 TEASPOON BAKING POWDER/BI-CARB OF SODA
½ CUP MILK
½ CUP WATER
1 CUP EXTRA PLAIN FLOUR

Sift the flour, salt and baking powder together into a bowl.

Make a well in the centre then gradually whisk in the milk and water. Coat your fish in extra flour and then dip in to the batter.

Tempura

1 EGG
1 CUP ICY COLD WATER
¾ CUP PLAIN FLOUR
PINCH BAKING POWDER/BI-CARBONATE OF SODA

Whisk the egg and water together. Add the flour and bi-carb and whisk to combine. Don't overbeat the mixture.

Beer

1½ CUPS PLAIN FLOUR
½ TEASPOON SALT
SALT AND PEPPER, TO SEASON
1 CAN/STUBBY (330-375ML) LIGHT BEER
1 CUP EXTRA PLAIN FLOUR

Sift the flour and salt together into a bowl. Season then make a well in the centre. Whisk in the beer gradually. Coat your fish in extra flour and then dip into the batter.

Soda Water

I have tried two versions of this. The first is quicker than the other, therefore I tend to use it more often!

#1 (quicker)

I CUP FLOUR

PINCH SALT

2 TEASPOONS BUTTER, MELTED

I CUP SODA WATER

Sift the flour and salt together into a bowl. Mix the butter through the flour and salt. Gradually whisk in the soda water.

#2

I CUP FLOUR

PINCH SALT

2 EGGS

60G MELTED BUTTER

I CUP SODA WATER

Sift the flour and salt together in a bowl. Add one egg and one lightly whisked egg yolk (reserve the egg white for later), the butter and soda water. Whisk together to combine. Allow to stand for 1 hour. Whisk the remaining egg white till stiff. Fold through the batter mixture.

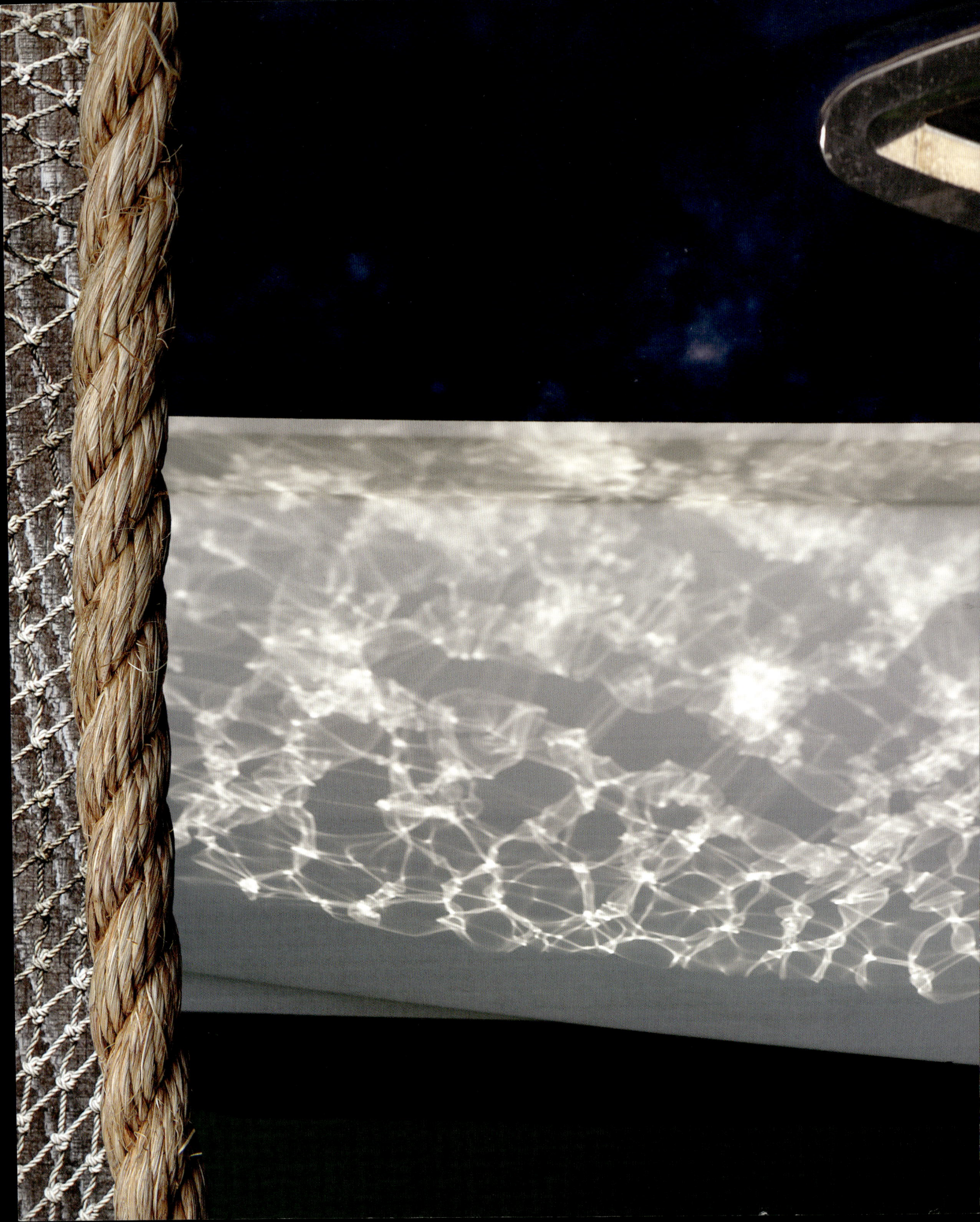

ASIAN
INFLUENCED

Teriyaki and Sweet Chilli Steamed Fish

4 FISH FILLETS
2 TABLESPOONS TERIYAKI
  SAUCE
1 TABLESPOON SWEET CHILLI
  SAUCE
½ TEASPOON SESAME OIL
1 CLOVE GARLIC, FINELY
  SLICED
1 LONG RED CHILLI,
  DESEEDED AND FINELY
  DICED
2 TABLESPOONS FRIED
  SHALLOTS OR ONIONS
  (AVAILABLE IN THE ASIAN
  SECTION OF SUPERMARKET)
RICE, COOKED, TO SERVE
BOK CHOY, TO SERVE

Place fish in a shallow dish. Combine teriyaki, sweet chilli, oil and garlic together and pour over fish. Leave to marinate for 10 minutes.

Place the fish on a plate and put in a bamboo steamer over simmering water. Steam for 4 to 5 minutes or until cooked through. The fish should flake apart with a fork when ready. Garnish with the chilli and fried shallots. Serve with rice and steamed bok choy on the side.

Serves 4

Ginger and Soy Steamed Fish

4 FISH FILLETS

1 TABLESPOON LIGHT SOY
  SAUCE

1 TEASPOON SESAME OIL

2 TABLESPOONS GINGER,
  GRATED

4 SPRING ONIONS, FINELY
  SLICED

¼ CUP CORIANDER LEAVES,
  CHOPPED

Place fish in a shallow dish. Combine soy, oil and ginger together and pour over fish. Leave to marinate for 10 minutes.

Place the fish on a plate and scatter the spring onions over the top. Put in a bamboo steamer over simmering water. Steam for 4 to 5 minutes or until cooked through. The fish should flake apart with a fork when ready. Serve garnished with coriander.

Serves 4

Ginger Steamed Fish

Slice each fish fillet into 4 pieces and lay in a shallow dish. Combine the wine, salt and pepper and pour over the fish. Leave to marinate for 10 minutes.

Place the fish on a plate and scatter the ginger over the top. Put in a bamboo steamer over simmering water. Steam for 4 to 5 minutes or until cooked through. The fish should flake apart with a fork when ready. Drizzle with the sesame oil and garnish with onions and coriander. Serve with steamed bok choy on the side.

Serves 4

4 FISH FILLETS
1½ TABLESPOONS SHAOXING
 WINE
SALT AND WHITE PEPPER
8CM PIECE GINGER,
 JULIENNED
2 TEASPOONS SESAME OIL
3 SPRING ONIONS, FINELY
 SLICED
¼ CUP CORIANDER LEAVES,
 ROUGHLY CHOPPED
BOK CHOY, TO SERVE

Coriander, Lime and Chilli Steamed Fish

Place fish in a shallow dish. Combine lime juice, rind, fish sauce, brown sugar and chilli. Pour over the fish, cover and marinate for 10 minutes.

Place the fish on a plate, top with coriander and mint. Put in a bamboo steamer over simmering water. Steam for 4 to 5 minutes or until cooked. Serve garnished with extra coriander leaves.

Serves 4

4 FISH FILLETS
1 LIME, ZESTED AND JUICED
1 TABLESPOON FISH SAUCE
1 TEASPOON BROWN SUGAR
1 LONG RED CHILLI,
  DESEEDED AND FINELY
  DICED
2 TABLESPOONS CORIANDER,
  FINELY CHOPPED
2 TABLESPOONS MINT, FINELY
  CHOPPED
EXTRA CORIANDER LEAVES

Asian-style Poached Fish

1 CUP COCONUT CREAM

1 CUP CHICKEN STOCK

10CM PIECE LEMONGRASS,
 BRUISED

5CM PIECE GINGER, GRATED

2 TABLESPOONS CORIANDER
 ROOT AND STEM, ROUGHLY
 CHOPPED

2 TABLESPOONS FISH SAUCE

2 TABLESPOONS BROWN
 SUGAR

4 FISH FILLETS

150G FRESH BABY CORN

COOKED BASMATI RICE

FRESH CORIANDER LEAVES

Combine coconut cream, stock, lemongrass, ginger, coriander root and stem, fish sauce and brown sugar in a saucepan. Bring to boil and then reduce to a simmer. Add fish and corn and cook for about 10 to 15 minutes, until fish breaks apart easily. Remove lemongrass from pan. Serve on a bed of rice, garnished with fresh coriander.

VARIATION
Remove fish from poaching juices and allow to cool. Serve wrapped in rice paper with lettuce and coriander and a sweet chilli dipping sauce.

Serves 4

Sticky Fish on Broccolini

This has to be my favourite Asian dish. I love the flavour, and it is easy to cook.

Heat oil and cook fish for approximately 3 minutes. Add garlic to the pan and cook for a further minute. Remove fish and drain on absorbent paper. Add sugar, fish sauce and lime leaves to pan and bring to the boil. Reduce heat and simmer for about 2 minutes or until thickened. Return fish to the pan with half the shallots and half the peanuts. Cook uncovered for 2 minutes, until mixture is sticky but not too dry.

Meanwhile boil, steam or microwave broccolini until just tender.

Stir 1 cup coriander leaves into cooked fish mince with lime juice and remaining shallots and peanuts. Place broccolini on platter, top with fish mix, remaining coriander and chilli.

Serves 4

1 TABLESPOON PEANUT OIL
300G FISH, MINCED
2 CLOVES GARLIC, SLICED
  THINLY
½ CUP PALM SUGAR, GRATED
2 TABLESPOONS FISH SAUCE
4 KAFFIR LIME LEAVES,
  SHREDDED
½ CUP DEEP FRIED SHALLOTS
  (FROM THE SUPERMARKET,
  ASIAN SECTION)
½ CUP TOASTED PEANUTS,
  CHOPPED
2 BUNCHES BROCCOLINI,
  HALVED LENGTHWAYS
1¼ CUPS CORIANDER LEAVES
1 TABLESPOON LIME JUICE
1 LONG RED CHILLI,
  DESEEDED AND THINLY
  SLICED

Deep-fried Whole Fish with a Thai Sauce

1 LONG RED CHILLI, DESEEDED
  AND FINELY SLICED

1 BUNCH CORIANDER, STEMS
  AND ROOTS ONLY

2 CLOVES GARLIC, FINELY
  CHOPPED

2CM PIECE GINGER, FINELY
  CHOPPED

4 KAFFIR LIME LEAVES, FINELY
  CHOPPED

2 TABLESPOONS FISH SAUCE

1 HEAPED TEASPOON BROWN
  SUGAR

2 LIMES, JUICED

3 SPRING ONIONS, FINELY SLICED

1 MEDIUM-SIZED WHOLE FISH
  (SUCH AS SNAPPER), GUTTED,
  SCALED AND CLEANED

2 EXTRA LIMES, JUICED

1 TABLESPOON SEA SALT

1 CUP RICE FLOUR

VEGETABLE OIL TO DEEP FRY

½ CUP CORIANDER LEAVES,
  ROUGHLY CHOPPED

½ CUP BASIL LEAVES, ROUGHLY
  CHOPPED

In a mortar and pestle (or food processor) blend together the chilli, coriander stem and roots, garlic, ginger, lime leaves, fish sauce and brown sugar. Once you have a rough paste remove to small bowl, add the lime juice and spring onions and combine. Put aside.

Score each side of the fish with 3 to 4 diagonal slices with a sharp knife. Pour over the fish the remaining lime juice and rub inside the fish with some sea salt. Coat the fish in rice flour.

Heat enough vegetable oil to fill two-thirds of a wok (maximum—see tip below). When oil is hot slide the whole fish in and cook for 5 to 7 minutes on each side.

Drain on absorbent paper. Move to serving platter, pour sauce over the top and scatter with coriander and basil leaves.

TIP: Please don't overfill the wok with oil as you are putting a whole fish into it and it could overflow. This can be so dangerous, so please be careful and don't get distracted!

Serves 2

Lemongrass Stir-fry with Toasted Coconut

1 STALK LEMONGRASS, FINELY
  CHOPPED

3 KAFFIR LIME LEAVES, SHREDDED

2 GARLIC CLOVES, FINELY
  CHOPPED

3CM PIECE GINGER, GRATED

1 LONG RED CHILLI, DE-SEEDED
  AND FINELY SLICED

1 LIME, JUICED

2 TABLESPOONS BROWN SUGAR

1 TABLESPOON FISH SAUCE

½ CUP SHREDDED COCONUT

2 TEASPOONS SESAME OIL

4 FISH FILLETS, THINLY SLICED

1 RED ONION, CUT INTO WEDGES

1 CARROT, JULIENNED

100G GREEN BEANS, TRIMMED
  AND HALVED

1 DOZEN PRAWNS, HEADS AND
  SHELLS REMOVED, TAILS LEFT
  ON (OPTIONAL)

2 CUPS COCONUT CREAM

1 CUP BEAN SPROUTS

1 CUP CORIANDER LEAVES,
  ROUGHLY CHOPPED

1 CUP MINT LEAVES, ROUGHLY
  CHOPPED

LIME WEDGES, TO SERVE

Blend the lemongrass, lime leaves, garlic, ginger, chilli, lime juice, brown sugar and fish sauce in a mortar and pestle, or blend in food processor, to form a paste.

Over a medium heat, heat up a wok. Add the coconut and cook, tossing for 2 minutes, or until lightly toasted. When cooked transfer to a bowl. Add oil to the wok and cook fish and onion in batches for about 2 minutes, or until lightly browned and cooked. When cooked transfer to a bowl. Add the paste to the wok and stir-fry for 1 minute. Add the carrot and beans, and stir-fry for 1 minute. Add the fish, onion and prawns, if using. Pour in the coconut cream and cook for 2 to 3 minutes until the sauce thickens.

Remove from the heat and add the bean sprouts, coriander and mint. Toss to combine. Divide among plates and sprinkle with toasted coconut and serve with lime wedges.

TIP: You can also toast the coconut under your grill. Line a baking tray with tin foil, spread the coconut evenly over the foil and place under the grill. Keep an eye on it and give it a toss occasionally. When it is nice and golden remove and allow to cool down.

Sweet and Sour Fish

Place kingfish pieces into a bowl with rice flour and coat evenly. Refrigerate until ready to deep fry them.

In a large saucepan, heat the vegetable oil to deep-fry the fish.

In another frypan heat the tablespoon of vegetable oil. Add capsicum, carrot and chilli and cook, over a moderate heat, for 2 to 4 minutes. IN a bowl, combine balsamic, soy, brown sugar and tomato paste and whisk. Add to the frypan of vegies and bring it all to the boil. Reduce the heat and simmer, stirring occasionally for 5 minutes.

Once the oil is ready, deep-fry the kingfish in batches for about 3 minutes until golden brown and drain on paper towel. Serve fish on rice, spoon over the sauce and garnish with spring onions and fresh coriander.

Serves 6

ASIAN INFLUENCED

4 KINGFISH FILLETS, IN 2CM CHUNKS

½ CUP RICE FLOUR

VEGETABLE OIL FOR DEEP-FRYING

I TABLESPOON VEGETABLE OIL EXTRA

I GREEN CAPSICUM, ROUGHLY CHOPPED

I CARROT, ROUGHLY CHOPPED

I LONG RED CHILLI, THINLY SLICED

I/3 CUP WHITE BALSAMIC VINEGAR

¼ CUP SOY SAUCE

2½ TABLESPOONS BROWN SUGAR

2 TABLESPOONS TOMATO PASTE

2 SPRING ONIONS, FINELY SLICED

½ BUNCH CORIANDER, FINELY CHOPPED

BASMATI RICE, COOKED, TO SERVE

FISHY FUN AND PICNICS

Fish Tacos

We have been having fish tacos for years, it's just another way we serve fish in a fun way for our kids! It is only recently that I found out that they are quite popular in California. This is our favourite way to prepare them.

Place fish fillets in a shallow dish. Sprinkle with lime rind, taco spice blend and salt. Top with coriander and lime juice and refrigerate for 2 hours.

Meanwhile, place lettuce, tomato and cheese in separate serving bowls. Add the balsamic to the tomatoes. Combine all sauce ingredients and stir well. Preheat oven and heat taco shells (and/or my favourite, tortillas) as per packet directions.

Heat oil and cook your fish on the barbecue (or in frypan). When cooked chop up, and place in a serving bowl. Serve everything in bowls on the table and everyone can make their own tacos or tortilla wraps!

Serves 6 (enough for roughly 2 tacos each)

4-6 FISH FILLETS (ROUGHLY 1 FILLET PER PERSON UNLESS THEY ARE LARGE FILLETS)
1 LIME, JUICED AND RIND GRATED
1 PACKET TACO SPICE BLEND (COMES IN THE BOX WITH THE TACOS)
SEA SALT
½ CUP CORIANDER, ROUGHLY CHOPPED
½ HEAD LETTUCE, SLICED
4 ROMA TOMATOES, DICED
1 CUP GRATED TASTY CHEESE
1 TABLESPOON BALSAMIC VINEGAR
12 TACO SHELLS OR TORTILLAS
2 TABLESPOONS OLIVE OIL

SAUCE

300ML SOUR CREAM
125G NATURAL YOGHURT
1 LIME, JUICED
PINCH SALT
3 CLOVES GARLIC, CRUSHED

Satay Fish Balls

You will need approximately 12 skewers, soaked in water, for this recipe.

850G FISH MINCE
5 SPRING ONIONS, FINELY
   SLICED
3CM PIECE GINGER, PEELED
   AND GRATED
2 TO 3 GARLIC CLOVES,
   CRUSHED
1 CUP BREADCRUMBS
1/3 CUP CORIANDER, FINELY
   CHOPPED
SALT AND PEPPER

SPRAY OIL
THAI SATAY SAUCE

Preheat oven to 200°C. Combine the fish mince, onions, ginger, garlic, breadcrumbs and coriander in a bowl. Season with salt and pepper and mix well. Roll into small balls of about 1 tablespoon mixture per each ball. Place on a tray, cover and put in the fridge until needed.

To serve on a skewer:
Thread 3 fish balls onto each skewer. Place on a baking tray lined with baking paper. Spray with oil and bake for 20 minutes until cooked and golden brown. Serve with satay sauce.

To serve as party food:
Place on a baking tray lined with baking paper. Spray with oil and bake for 20 minutes until cooked and golden brown. Serve with toothpicks and satay sauce on side.

Serves 4

Fish Pate

I love this pate which uses my preserved fish (see page 186), or at a close second, smoked fish (see page 183).

Blend all the ingredients, except the cream, in a food processor until well combined. Add cream slowly into the processor at the end.

Serve in bowls with warm Turkish bread slices.

200G FISH (PRESERVED OR
 SMOKED)
250G CREAM CHEESE
2 TABLESPOONS MAYONNAISE
2 TABLESPOONS DILL, FINELY
 CHOPPED
1 TABLESPOON DIJON
 MUSTARD
½ LEMON, JUICED
¼ TEASPOON WHITE PEPPER
1 SPRING ONION, CHOPPED
1 TEASPOON CAPERS
1 TABLESPOON CREAM
 (OPTIONAL)

Fish Pasties

Combine the fish and 1 tablespoon of the hoisin sauce in a bowl. Cover and refrigerate for 15 minutes. Heat the oil in a frypan over a medium-high heat. Add the fish, onion and ginger and cook, stirring, for 3 to 4 minutes then add the mixed vegies, capsicum and the remaining hoisin sauce. Cook for a further 4 minutes. Remove from the heat, stir through the spring onion and coriander and let cool.

Preheat the oven to 220°C. Line a baking tray with baking paper.

Using a large pastry cutter (about 10cm diameter) cut out 4 rounds per sheet of pastry. Brush the edges of the circle with egg and place a tablespoon of the mixture in the centre. Fold the pastry over in half and use a fork to press the edges together. Place finished pasties on the baking tray, brush lightly with more egg and sprinkle with the sesame seeds. Bake in the oven for 10-15 minutes or until nice and golden in colour.

TIP: If you want to freeze these for later or are making them a day or two ahead of time, cook only till just golden, then refrigerate or freeze. Simply defrost or bring to room temperature and bake in oven to heat.

Makes 16 pasties

FILLING

300G FISH, MINCED

2 TABLESPOONS HOISIN SAUCE

3 TEASPOONS SESAME OIL

1 SMALL BROWN ONION, FINELY DICED

2CM PIECE GINGER, GRATED

1 CUP FROZEN DICED MIXED VEGIES

1/3 CUP RED CAPSICUM, FINELY DICED

2 SPRING ONIONS, FINELY CHOPPED

¼ CUP CORIANDER, FINELY CHOPPED

4 SHEETS FROZEN PUFF PASTRY

1 EGG, LIGHTLY BEATEN

1 TABLESPOON SESAME SEEDS

Fish Finger Croquettes

BÉCHAMEL SAUCE
20G BUTTER
2 TABLESPOONS PLAIN FLOUR
I CUP MILK

2 TABLESPOONS OLIVE OIL
500G FISH, CUT INTO SMALL
  CUBES
2 GARLIC CLOVES, CRUSHED
I SMALL BROWN ONION,
  FINELY DICED

1½ CUPS EXTRA PLAIN FLOUR
3 EGGS, LIGHTLY BEATEN
2 CUPS BREADCRUMBS
VEGETABLE OIL FOR DEEP
  FRYING

To make the béchamel sauce, melt the butter in a small saucepan over a medium heat. Add the flour and cook, stirring, for one minute. Remove from the heat and gradually whisk in the milk. Put back on the heat and cook, whisking constantly, until sauce thickens.

Make the croquettes: in a frypan, heat olive oil. Add fish, garlic and onion and cook over a medium heat for 4 to 5 minutes or until fish is cooked. Transfer to a processor and blend. Spoon into a bowl and combine with the béchamel sauce. Mix well and season with salt and pepper. Cover and refrigerate for a couple of hours, or until chilled.

Now for the messy part, I like to coat my hands in flour lightly to help, but either way be prepared to get sticky!

Have the extra flour, eggs and breadcrumbs arranged on 3 separate plates. Also, have a baking tray lined with baking paper ready.

Take approximately 1 tablespoon of mixture and shape it into a 'finger' or into balls if you prefer. Roll in flour, dip in egg and roll in breadcrumbs firmly to coat. (Keep your hands damp to avoid the stickiness of the flour.) Place on a baking tray. When all are complete, cover the tray and refrigerate for about 15 to 20 minutes until firm.

Pour vegetable oil into a large saucepan, until about 1/3 full. Heat over a medium heat until hot. (Test with a piece of bread, the oil is hot enough if the bread sizzles). Cook the fish fingers in batches of 4 or 5 for about 2 minutes or until they are golden in colour. Transfer to plate to drain on absorbent paper. Serve with mashed potatoes and peas or a good old serving of fries.

TIP: Add some canned corn kernels (drained) and some chives to the mix.

Fish Bites

These are similar to sausage rolls.

¼ CUP BREADCRUMBS

2 TABLESPOONS MILK

300G FISH

½ ONION, CUT INTO WEDGES

½ BABY FENNEL BULB,
  ROUGHLY CHOPPED

1 LARGE GARLIC CLOVE

1 EGG

1 BUNCH CORIANDER, FINELY
  CHOPPED

½ CUP DILL, FINELY CHOPPED

2 SHEETS PUFF PASTRY

1 EXTRA EGG, LIGHTLY
  BEATEN

Preheat oven to 220°C and line a baking tray with paper.

In a large mixing bowl combine breadcrumbs and milk. Chop fish into smallish cubes and mince in a food processor. Add onion, fennel and garlic to the processor. Once minced add to the bowl of breadcrumb mix. Stir in egg, coriander and dill. Now get messy and mix well with your hands.

Lay out sheet of pastry. Cut in half lengthways. Place a small quantity of fish mixture in a row along the length of the pastry.

Brush edges lightly with extra egg. Roll up the pastry and cut into bite size lengths. Brush with egg and place on a lined baking tray.

Repeat process until all mixture is used.

Bake in oven for 15 to 20 minutes or until golden brown.

Makes about 18

Smoked Fish

This is actually Al, my husband's recipe, he loves smoking his catch. He will smoke the fish and vacuum seal it in smaller quantities. This allows us to store it for longer. Tuna and marlin are amongst his favourites to smoke. We bought a small metal box smoker and it works a treat, it is also very easy and to start you off it comes complete with the sawdust you require. Some people also smoke fish on their barbecue, using the tray underneath as the smoker and the hood as the cover.

Combine the water with the sugar, salt and chillies. Pour the mix over the fish making sure the fish is completely covered. Place into a large air-tight container with the lid on and refrigerate for at least 24 hours.

A smoker is basically divided up into 3 levels. The bottom is where you put the sawdust or hickory chips, depending on what you use, then there are two wire racks, a bottom one and a top one. We generally cook on the top tray as it is quicker, but the two trays allow you to cook more.

When ready to smoke, put a small pile of sawdust in your smoker and spread it out over the centre of the bottom. Put the wire trays in, placing your fish on the top wire rack. Put the lid on and place the smoker over the lit fuel. 1 kilogram of fish will take approximately 15 to 20 minutes. Don't overcook it, or it will become chewy. It is ready when it goes a golden brown colour.

TIP: Smaller fish such as trout, tailor and trevally can be smoked whole, you will need to gut and clean the insides and be sure to remove all traces of blood. Even if your local fish monger guts and cleans for you, I would suggest you give it a good wash before drying it. Then the fish is ready to soak in the brine and smoke.

Remember when smoking the whole fish that there will be bones, so care must be taken to remove them if using the fish in other recipes.

1KG FISH, FILLETED

BRINE
ENOUGH WATER TO COVER
1 TABLESPOON COOKING SALT
¾ CUP BROWN SUGAR
2 LONG RED CHILLIES, DE-
SEEDED AND FINELY SLICED

*This page: Honey vinaigrette yabbies (see page 141)
and preserved fish in jars (see page 186). Opposite:
Smoked tailor. (see page 183).*

Preserved Tuna

STAGE ONE

2 LITRES WATER

2 CELERY STICKS (WITH
  LEAVES), CUT INTO PIECES

2 CLOVES GARLIC

3 BAY LEAVES

3 CLOVES

1 LARGE BROWN ONION, CUT
  INTO WEDGES

1 TEASPOON PEPPERCORNS

3-4 TEASPOONS (COOKING)
  SALT

1KG TUNA

VARIATION #1
BAY LEAF AND THYME

1 LITRE OLIVE OIL

200ML GRAPE SEED OIL

5 FRESH BAY LEAVES

1 BUNCH FRESH THYME

1 TEASPOON PEPPERCORNS

2 BIRDS EYE CHILLIES, I LIKE
  TO EITHER SLICE DOWN ONE
  SIDE OF THEM OR FINELY
  SLICE THEM UP TO ALLOW
  MORE FLAVOUR INTO THE OIL

Because we are a canned-tuna-free house, I wanted to find a way that would allow me to get the same result at home with minimal effort. After loads of research (including the old way of salting) I ended up with the method below. I wanted something that wasn't going to take days to do and all up it takes just bits and pieces of my time for a day. It is well worth it, I keep the jars in the fridge and pull them out to get to room temperature when I want to use them. The three variations below are my favourite flavours, but the beauty of it is you can use what you like best.

This is what I use whenever a recipe calls for canned tuna, it goes great in pasta, quiche and frittata, on pizza, in dips, pates and salads and also when stuffing capsicums or mushrooms. Give it a go, you won't be disappointed!

STAGE ONE

Put all the ingredients for stage one except the tuna in a large saucepan and bring to the boil. Boil for 30 minutes. Reduce heat to low, add tuna and cook for about 15 minutes. As with most fish this cooking time will depend on how thick you cut your tuna.

Turn off the heat and let it cool for about 3 hours in the pot.

STAGE TWO

Put tuna in a large preserving jar. Top with oils and ingredients, from one of either of my three recipes below or one of your own. Leave for 48 hours in the refrigerator. When you are going to use the preserved fish just bring it back to room temperature.

TIP: I like to put my tuna in a few smaller jars, this allows me to use a range of flavours each time rather than just one. To do this I work on the ratio of 1:5 with the grapeseed oil to olive oil. I also lessen the quantities of the other ingredients to suit the size of the jar.

I have tried this with kingfish as well and it came up beautifully.

I find I need to put the fish on absorbent towel straight from the jar to drain excess oil when I am going to use it.

VARIATION #2
GINGER AND LIME

1 LITRE OLIVE OIL

200ML GRAPE SEED OIL

5CM PIECE GINGER, FINELY
  JULIENNED

1 LIME, PEELED AND RIND
  FINELY SLICED

1 BIRDS EYE CHILLI, FINELY
  SLICED

VARIATION #3
LEMON AND DILL

1 LITRE OLIVE OIL

200ML GRAPE SEED OIL

1 LEMON, PEELED AND RIND
  FINELY SLICED.

½ BUNCH FRESH DILL,
  FINELY CHOPPED

1 TEASPOON WHOLE
  PEPPERCORNS

Smoked Fish Sandwich Fingers

250G SMOKED FISH (SEE PAGE 183), FLAKED
200G CREAMED CHEESE
2 TABLESPOONS DILL, FINELY CHOPPED
1 TABLESPOON CAPERS, FINELY CHOPPED
1 CLOVE GARLIC, CRUSHED
1 LEMON, ZESTED AND JUICED
SALT AND PEPPER, TO SEASON
8 SLICES OF BREAD, CRUSTS REMOVED
2 LEBANESE CUCUMBERS, CUT IN HALF AND THINLY SLICED LENGTHWAYS

Combine the fish, cheese, dill, capers, garlic, lemon rind and juice.

Mix well and season to taste. Divide the fish mixture between 4 slices of the bread. Top with cucumber and remaining bread and cut into fingers.

TIP: This mix is great to use in baguettes or wraps as well.

Remember if you are using a whole smoked fish to make sure you remove all the bones from the flesh before using!!

Makes 12 finger sandwiches

Clockwise from front: Smoked fish sandwich fingers; Fish and dill savoury tarts; Fish bites; Kingfish and asparagus frittata; pear, fig and kingfish tart; fish pate; Satay fish balls.

Know your fish

	Flesh colour	Composition of flesh	Cooking suggestions	Al's table rating
Albacore	Pale Pink	Relatively firm, dry	Fillet, Cutlet	EXCELLENT
Australian Salmon	Pale Pink to Brown	Firm, dry	Whole, Fillet, Cutlet	CRAP
Bait Yellowtail, Slimy Mackerel	Pale Pink	Relatively firm	Whole, Fillet	REASONABLE
Barramundi	White	Soft, delicate	Whole, Fillet, Cutlet	EXCELLENT
Black Jewfish	White	Soft/flakey	Fillet, Cutlet	EXCELLENT
Bluefin Tuna	Red	Firm	Fillet, Cutlet	EXCELLENT
Bonefish		NOT RECOMMENDED		
Bonito—Austtralian, Watsons Leaping	Pink	Soft	Whole, Fillet, Cutlet	REASONABLE
Bream—Black, Yellowfin, Pikey	White	Relatively firm, fine texture	Whole, Fillet	REASONABLE
Cobia	Pink	Firm	Fillet, Cutlet	GOOD
Coral Trout	White	White moist flesh, firm	Whole, Fillet	EXCELLENT
Dolphinfish (Mahi-Mahi)	Pink	Relatively firm	Whole, Fillet	EXCELLENT
Estuary Cod	White	Relatively firm	Fillet	REASONABLE
Estuary Perch	White	Soft	Whole, Fillet	REASONABLE
Flathead—Sand, Dusky, Tiger	White	Dry firm flesh	Whole, Fillet	EXCELLENT
Giant Trevally	White	Firm	Whole, Fillet	EXCELLENT
Golden Snapper	Pink	Relatively firm	Whole, Fillet	EXCELLENT
Jewfish	Pink	Soft/flakey	Fillet, Cutlet	GOOD

Fish	Colour	Texture	Cuts	Rating
John Dory	White	White moist flesh, firm	Whole, Fillet	EXCELLENT
Leatherjackets	White	Firm	Whole	GOOD
Longtail Tuna	Red	Relatively firm	Fillet	GOOD
Mackerel Tuna	Red	Soft	Fillet	CRAP
Mangrove Jack	White	Relatively firm	Whole, Fillet	EXCELLENT
Marlin—Striped, Blue, Black	Pink	Firm	Cutlets, Steaks	REASONABLE
Morwong	White	Firm and moist	Whole, Fillet	REASONABLE
Pink Ling	Pale Pink to White	Soft	Fillet	GOOD
Queenfish	Pink	Relatively firm	Fillet	REASONABLE
Sailfish		NOT RECOMMENDED		
Samson fish	Pink	Firm	Small fish best whole	
Silver Trevally	White	Firm	Whole, Fillet	REASONABLE
Snapper	Pink	Medium and moist	Whole, Fillet, Cutlet	GOOD
Spanish Mackerel	White	Relatively firm	Fillet, Cutlet	GOOD
Squid—Calamari, Arrow	White	Firm	Rings, Pieces or Stuffed	EXCELLENT
Striped Tuna	Red	Firm	Fillet, Cutlet	CRAP
Swordfish	Pink	Firm	Cutlets, Steaks	EXCELLENT
Tailor	White	Soft	Whole, Fillet	REASONABLE
Threadfin Salmon/Blue Salmon	White	Soft	Fillet, Cutlet	EXCELLENT
Wahoo	Pink	Firm	Fillet, Cutlet	EXCELLENT
Whiting—King George, Sand	White	Delicate	Whole, Fillet	EXCELLENT
Yellowfin Tuna	Red	Firm	Fillet, Cutlet	EXCELLENT
Yellowtail Kingfish	Pink	Firm	Whole, Fillet, Cutlet	EXCELLENT

First published in Australia in 2010 by
New Holland Publishers (Australia) Pty Ltd
Sydney • Auckland • London • Cape Town

1/66 Gibbes Street Chatswood NSW 2067 Australia
218 Lake Road Northcote Auckland New Zealand
86 Edgware Road London W2 2EA United Kingdom
Wembley Square First Floor Solan Road Gardens Cape Town 8001 South Africa

A record of this book is held at the National Library of Australia

ISBN 9781742574073 (pbk)
ISBN 9781741109542 (hdbk)

Publisher: Fiona Schultz
Publishing Manager: Lliane Clarke
Editor: Kay Proos
Proofreader: Geraldine Coren
Designer: Tania Gomes
Photographs: Graeme Gillies/NHIL
Family photographs: Al McGlashan
Cover photograph: Graeme Gillies/NHIL
Food styling: Rachel McGlashan and Graeme Gillies
Production Manager: Olga Dementiev
Printer: Toppan Leefung Printing Ltd (China)

10 9 8 7 6 5 4 3 2 1

www.thefishwife.com.au
www.almcglashan.com
www.newhollandpublishers.com